W9-BAM-895

FRANCE 1940

FRANCE
1940
DEFENDING THE REPUBLIC

PHILIP NORD

YALE UNIVERSITY PRESS
NEW HAVEN AND LONDON

For information about this and other Yale University Press publications, please contact:
U.S. Office: sales.press@yale.edu   www.yalebooks.com
Europe Office: sales@yaleup.co.uk   www.yalebooks.co.uk

Typeset in Adobe Caslon Pro by IDSUK (DataConnection) Ltd
Printed in Great Britain by TJ International Ltd, Padstow, Cornwall

Nord, Philip G., 1950-
    France 1940 : defending the republic / Philip Nord.
        pages cm
    Includes bibliographical references and index.
    ISBN 978-0-300-18987-2 (cl : alk. paper)
 1. World War, 1939–1945—Campaigns—France.   I. Title.
    D755.2.N67 2015
    940.54'214—dc23

                                                                    2014047023

A catalogue record for this book is available from the British Library.

10 9 8 7 6 5 4 3 2 1

FSC MIX
Paper from
responsible sources
FSC® C013056
www.fsc.org

In memory of my father

CONTENTS

ACKNOWLEDGMENTS

I owe a special debt of gratitude to two Princeton colleagues, Paul Miles and Steven Kotkin, who read the manuscript through from beginning to end. Their informed counsel toughened up the argument and saved me from all too many mistakes. I also had occasion to turn for help to Claire Andrieu and David Cannadine, who were generous with their time and expertise. This project got under way while I was a Florence Gould Fellow at the National Humanities Center in North Carolina. My thanks to the NHC for affording me the opportunity to explore a path I would not have otherwise explored. My warm thanks also to my editors at Yale University Press: Heather McCallum, whose encouragement and guidance were essential to bringing the project to fruition; and

ACKNOWLEDGMENTS

Richard Mason, who went over the manuscript with an experienced eye, ironing out inconsistencies and helping to unsnarl my prose. As always, I can't see how I would have managed any of this without the steadying hand and loving partnership of my wife, Deborah. She is the best.

STRANGE DEFEAT?

There have been many wars and many defeats, but France's defeat in 1940 was among the most momentous in Europe's history. France, not twenty years before, had emerged a victor in the Great War, its army as a result earning a reputation as one of the strongest in the world. That war had ground on for more than four years. The campaign of 1940 by contrast was over in a comparative twinkling after just six weeks of combat, and the result was a rout. An estimated 90,000 French soldiers died in the fighting and well over a million and a half were taken prisoner. France's parliament gave up on democratic institutions and turned over the reins of power to a military man, Marshal Philippe Pétain, who proceeded to construct an authoritarian regime that entered into collaboration with Hitler's Germany.

The Führer's tank commander, Heinz Guderian, was astounded by Germany's lightning victory over France, calling it nothing less than a "miracle."[1] The accumulating misfortunes, though, were not France's alone. The British, Soviets, and Americans had all predicated their own defense policies on the sure-fire staying power of the French army and now had to scramble to recalibrate their plans. Hitler in the meantime was unleashed on Europe, and it would take almost five years more of bitter warfare to bring him at last to heel.

A defeat of such dimensions—not just massive but also unexpected—cried out for explanation. Pétain, as might be imagined, had one ready to hand, which he articulated in a speech on 20 June, just four days after he had become prime minister and three after appealing to the Germans for an armistice: "Too few babies, too few arms, too few allies—these were the causes of our defeat," as he put it.[2] Marc Bloch had an account of his own, which he laid out with prosecutorial brilliance in *L'Etrange Défaite*, dashed off in 1940 while the wounds of the battlefield collapse were still fresh (although the text would not be published until after the war). Bloch had unkind words for France's British ally, complained of a shortage of weaponry, but most of all insisted on the lack of imagination of French military planners who, still under the spell of the Great War with its set-piece battles, had failed to grasp the speed of modern mechanized combat. Bloch did not stop there, though, but, like Pétain, shifted from military critique to social indictment. It wasn't, of course, demographic deficits that upset Bloch but the self-centered individualism of the French body politic, from the blinkered bourgeois down to the wage-grubbing trade unionist. A generalized selfishness had eaten into public life, draining away the Jacobin esprit de corps that Bloch so well embodied himself and that he believed to be the sine qua non of victory in war.[3]

For Pétain and Bloch, the defeat of 1940 was not just a military event but a moral judgment on France as a nation. Such a view had a long life ahead of it. *In Search of France*, a collection of half a dozen essays, was published in English and French editions in 1963.[4] The volume is and remains a classic, the product of a collaborative effort undertaken by top scholars, social scientists all, from Harvard and the Paris Institute of Political Studies (better known as Sciences Po). It does not deal in the specifics of the 1940 campaign, but it does present a picture of the France that went before, of a nation en route to defeat, and it is a devastating portrait. That France, the France of the Third Republic, is characterized as a "stalemate society," anchored by an alliance of conservative peasants and bourgeois committed to preserving the status quo. The Republic's parliamentary constitution, "plenty of brakes and not much of a motor," helped to keep change at bay, which was fine in the sunny days of the Belle Epoque, but not so fine in the Depression years when a France wedded to backward ways failed to modernize, when a risk-averse France failed to face the Nazi threat head-on. One of the book's contributors, Jean-Baptiste Duroselle, spoke of a "decline in France's *élan vital.*" He went on in later years to author a weighty tome, anatomizing French foreign policy in the 1930s, and he titled it with lapidary simplicity *La Décadence.* Duroselle was just as pithy when it came to characterizing the unavoidable outcome of decadence: catastrophe.[5] Now, *In Search of France* was a hopeful volume in the end. The catastrophe of 1940 and the years of Occupation that followed, the authors proposed, had incubated a generation of new men who, inheritors of power after the war, would set the nation on a modernizing course that promised a return to grandeur. This narrative of decline and renewal, with 1940 cast as the turning point, achieved wide currency in the 1960s. It was relayed to a general public (minus the renewal end of the story) in a pair of massive histories which recapitulated the received wisdom but framed it in compelling, readable prose that demanded the reader's assent: William Shirer's *The Collapse of the Third Republic* and Alistair Horne's *To Lose a Battle,* both, as it happens, published in 1969.[6]

The consensus, however, did not long endure. An alternative interpretation began to take shape in the 1970s that questioned the notion of a decadent France. It has picked up speed since, generating a flood of fresh material, and this new, revisionist view is now summed up in a couple of first-rate recent English-language histories: Ernest May's *Strange Victory* (2000) and Julian Jackson's *The Fall of France* (2003).[7]

These authors see effort where critics have seen abdication and bankruptcy. French diplomats may have been slow to catch on to the Nazi threat, but catch on they did, and they then labored hard to build an anti-German coalition, dragging along allies who were reluctant to abandon entrenched policies of appeasement and neutralism. Pétain and Bloch blamed the French defeat on too few arms. Not so, answer the revisionists, who counter that France's rearmament drive in the late 1930s—except in the domain of aircraft production and perhaps even in that domain too—was more success than failure. Nor was the French public so slack and pacifist as is oftentimes supposed. In the wake of the Munich debacle of 1938, opinion stiffened, rallying to the banner of national defense. As for the defeat itself, no doubt French soldiers were ill served by their generals, but they fought well nonetheless, and the military catastrophe that unfolded in May–June 1940 was due as much to what the Germans did right as to what the

French did wrong. Not just that: France went to war with allies. The "strange defeat" of 1940 was a defeat for them too—for the British, Belgians, and Dutch—so why read the event as a reflection on the French alone?

So, who is right? No definitive conclusion, of course, is possible, but I will make the case for a more sympathetic understanding of France's defeat.

This book is as much an argument as a narrative history, and unlike much of the work on the subject, it will set the French experience in a comparative perspective. There is a strong tendency to view France's fate in isolation. In many ways, to be sure, the 1930s were a "low dishonest decade" for the French, but they were that too for most of Europe. France was routed in the spring of 1940, but for Hitler's military the Battle of France was just one victory in an unbroken string (the Battle of Britain apart) that did not come to an end until the German army's advance ground to a halt outside Moscow in early December 1941. Add in the defeats dealt by the Japanese to Great Britain and the United States in the Pacific theater on into 1942—from Singapore to the Philippines—and France's own misfortunes begin to look a good deal less "strange." If France's debacle is proof of moral decay, then the entire non-fascist world must stand in the dock alongside. .

Yet in one crucial, even paramount, respect, France's defeat was exceptional, and the comparative perspective brings that aspect into sharp relief. In the aftermath of the 1940 debacle, the Dutch sovereign, Queen Wilhelmina, the Dutch government by her side, departed for exile in Britain. So too did the Belgian government, though the king, Leopold III, elected to stay behind. In France, just one government member made his way to London, Charles de Gaulle, and he was no more than a junior minister acting on his own initiative. It is not that the French government made no effort to continue the fight from abroad. There was an attempt to relocate the Republic's most senior officials to North Africa in June 1940, but that effort was sabotaged. No, the French government did not take the path of exile but transformed itself, step by step, into an authoritarian and collaborationist regime, Vichy.

This was a unique outcome, one that requires a France-specific explanation, and I will advance just such an explanation at the end of the book. Suffice it to say for the moment that Vichy's advent was not proof of French decadence but of another, no less consequential malaise whose diagnosis remains as yet to be worked out. Most discussions of 1940 stop with the armistice in June; this one will carry the story a month further to show how and why defeat ended in the Third Republic's demise and its replacement by the Vichy government of Philippe Pétain. In this respect, my account will be more encompassing than previous ones. While adding on a month to the story may not sound that consequential, it is, for in those few weeks a democracy, abetted by its enemies, self-destructed, a dispiriting spectacle that raises questions about the vulnerabilities of democratic institutions in France (as elsewhere for that matter).

Last of all, let's assume for a moment that the revisionists have got a persuasive case, that the story of France's defeat is one of military failure and not a commentary on the moral and political failings of the nation as a whole. Does such a finding have any bearing on the larger course of French history?

This book is divided into three parts, each composed of two chapters. The first part takes the story to 1939. The second focuses on the Battle of France itself, while the third deals with the political consequences of French defeat. I conclude with some general reflections on the final issue raised. What difference does it make that the Third Republic was not so rotten as often imagined and that the French, contrary to much received opinion, put up a creditable fight in 1940?

PART I

WAR PREPAREDNESS

CHAPTER 1

DIPLOMACY

"Too few babies, too few arms, too few allies": such was Pétain's first stab at accounting for France's defeat in 1940. That was in a radio address of 20 June, four days after he had become premier. Pétain made a second go of it five days later, once again in a radio speech, although this time he laid greater weight on the nation's moral failings: "Our defeat was due to our laxness. The spirit of pleasure-seeking brings to ruin what the spirit of sacrifice has built." And the Marshal's voice carried weight. Not only was he France's prime minister: he was the nation's greatest living war hero, the victor of Verdun, for France the costliest battle of the Great War. Demographics do not get the same play today as they did in Pétain's time, but otherwise, the explanation for France's collapse has not changed much since. France just wasn't ready to go to war.

In certain respects, France was indeed in "an unfavorable strategic situation" when the war began in September 1939.[1] In contrast to the Great War, there was not much of an Eastern Front to speak of. French diplomacy in the 1930s had flirted with a Soviet alliance but never followed through, hobbled by anti-communist apprehensions. The Soviets in the end gave up on the anti-fascist cause, signing a non-aggression pact with the Germans in August. France had made an effort to cultivate substitute eastern allies in Czechoslovakia and Poland, but that effort fell short. France sold out her Czechoslovak ally at Munich in September 1938, and the following March, Hitler swallowed up what remained of an independent Czechoslovakia. Britain answered back, promising to guarantee Polish territorial integrity against Nazi depredations, and the French took steps to reaffirm an already long-standing commitment to Poland. The two Allied powers made good their pledges when Hitler moved on Poland in September, but in the event France did little to supply the Poles with much substantive military assistance, in effect leaving them to fend for themselves. But even had the French wanted to do more, they faced a major logistical problem. Italy stood in the way between France and Poland, literally, and Italy was bound by alliance to the Germans. Rapprochement between the two dictatorships had begun in the fall of 1936, culminating in a full-fledged military alliance, the Pact of Steel, concluded in May 1939. The Rome–Berlin axis, as it came to be called, had not been an inevitability. In 1934 a Hitler still new to power had menaced Austria. Italy stood up to Hitler and forced him to back down, a show of resolve that led to a warming of relations between Italy, France, and Great Britain too. But the three-power entente that resulted, the Stresa Front, had been allowed to unravel, such that Mussolini (as Stalin would do later) deemed it wiser to make a deal with Hitler rather than to oppose him.

France, however, did have one friend among Europe's great powers, and that was Great Britain, but how difficult it had been to bring the British around. In March 1936, Hitler had remilitarized the Rhineland in contravention of the Versailles Treaty. The French contemplated action but took none, deterred in part by Britain's refusal to help out. Later that year, General Francisco Franco mounted a military coup against the Spanish Republic. France's Popular Front, led by the Socialist Léon Blum, wanted to come to the aid of its sister Republic but once again did little. Britain had made clear it would not stand by France in case of a war over Spain, and so Blum backed off, seeking instead to coax the interested powers—Germany, Italy, and the Soviet Union—to agree to non-intervention.

Yet for a third time, during the Munich crisis, the French bent to Britain's will. British Prime Minister Neville Chamberlain wanted to pursue a policy of appeasement, and the French, ever the junior partners, went along. Unkind critics have characterized Britain today as a "poodle," taking its lead from a bossy United States, but things were different in the 1930s. Then Britain was the imperious "governess" and France her sometime restive but on the whole compliant charge.[2]

So, yes, there is a strong case to be made that France's strategic position in 1939 was unfavorable. Just think about it in comparison to 1914. At that time, the Germans had faced a formidable Eastern Front opponent in Imperial Russia. In 1939 the Soviet Union was more co-conspirator than enemy. All that stood in the Germans' way was Poland, which had the pluck to put up a gallant fight but not the means to do more than that. In the Great War, Italy wound up on the side of the Entente. In the Second World War, it took Germany's part. Then there is Great Britain. It got into the Great War at the very last minute, but once in, it did not hold back, dispatching an initial expeditionary force of six divisions that ballooned to twenty within a year. In the run-up to the Second World War, Britain committed itself sooner (a commitment to send troops was firmed up in the wake of Munich, almost a year before the actual outbreak of hostilities) but in the event never mustered more than a smallish army for continental service—ten divisions in all as late as May 1940.[3] How was it that France found itself in such a predicament? For many historians, the answer is a simple one: bad policy, a diplomacy that was hesitant, short-sighted, and spineless.[4]

It is possible, however, to read France's diplomatic record in less negative terms. To be sure, it took precious time for French policy-makers to catch on to the nature of the Nazi threat, but they did in the end and took the lead in assembling an anti-German coalition, patching together the strongest alliance possible in conditions that were difficult, to say the least. And while the French may have been slow to grasp the true state of affairs, others were slower still, sticking to policies of appeasement and neutralism up to the last minute, if not beyond. This is not to say that the French themselves were blameless, not at all, just that there was plenty of guilt to go around and that the French don't deserve to be singled out.

It is not difficult to see why France took so long to face up to the Nazi threat. First of all, the French already had a policy in place to deal with the Germans—Briandism— that, into the early 1930s, appeared to be working just fine. At Locarno in 1925, France's Foreign Minister Aristide Briand had played a pivotal part in negotiating a series of international agreements that confirmed the basic tenets of the Versailles Treaty in the West. Germany itself was among the signatories. The Germans still harbored ambitions to revise the Versailles settlement in the East, but France built up a network of regional alliances there to deter any potential aggression. In the aftermath of Locarno, Germany was step by step rewoven into the fabric of international life. It joined the League of Nations in 1926. The Young Plan of 1929 readjusted German war reparations debts to a more manageable level. As the 1930s began, the French might well congratulate themselves that Germany, Gulliver-like, was enmeshed in a web of collective agreements of sufficient strength to hold its revisionist impulses in check.[5]

The Nazi seizure of power in January 1933 upset the order of things. With little delay, Hitler set about shredding the bonds that pinned Germany down. He pulled Germany out of the League in October. He threatened military intervention in Austria the following year and then in 1935 repudiated the provisions of the Versailles Treaty constraining German rearmament.

France, however, was not without an answer to such challenges. The "spirit of Locarno" was dead, but there was still the possibility of containing Germany through regional alliances and international pressure. France came to an agreement with Italy and Great Britain in April 1935, the Stresa Front, with the goal of guaranteeing

Austrian independence. Just weeks after that, France signed a mutual assistance pact with the Soviet Union, a reminder to the Germans that they were hemmed in on all sides. Containment and deterrence remained the order of the day in French policy, and for a moment the strategy seemed to work: Hitler backed down over Austria.

Then things began to come unstuck. Britain first of all went freelancing, working out a bilateral agreement with the Germans in June 1935 that regulated tonnage ratios between the two nations' navies. The British did not consult the French on the matter, making plain Britain's willingness to act alone in areas, like naval policy, where it felt that its vital interests were at stake.[6] More consequential still was the Ethiopian crisis. In October, Mussolini ordered the invasion of the independent and sovereign kingdom of Ethiopia, a barefaced and brutal territorial grab. The League of Nations imposed economic sanctions on the Italians, but to no avail. Behind the scenes, Britain and France maneuvered to find a negotiated way out of the imbroglio. In the interests of maintaining anti-German solidarity, however, they were at the same time anxious not to ruffle Mussolini, and so the Franco-British "solution" tilted toward the Italians, in effect rewarding them for aggression. When the terms of the deal were leaked to the press, the British dissociated themselves from it, at one and the same time leaving the French in the lurch and irritating the Italians. Italian policy henceforth began to veer away from Stresa Front solidarity. Then in the first week of March 1936 came yet more bad news. France and Belgium had signed a mutual defense pact in 1920, which the Belgian government now repudiated. It was internal politics that determined the decision. The centrist Van Zeeland government wanted to rearm, but it faced resistance from anti-militarist socialists and from anti-French Flemings. Abrogation of the 1920 treaty, it was hoped, would mollify opponents and smooth the path to an overhaul of the nation's military.[7]

This was the background to the Rhineland crisis. On 7 March 1936, the very day after Belgium pulled out of its partnership with the French, Hitler marched German troops into the Rhineland in violation of the Versailles Treaty. Who was in a position to come to France's material aid? Not the Italians, who were edging into the German orbit, an evolution consummated over the coming summer months by concerted German-Italian intervention in the Spanish Civil War. Not the Belgians, who had backed out of an alliance with France en route to a policy of neutralism. And not the British, who continued to view the French as troublemakers all too willing to snarl Britain in unwelcome continental entanglements. As for the international community, it had demonstrated its impotence during the Ethiopian affair (and would soon do so again in 1936 in its failure to enforce non-intervention in Spain). There was, of course, the option of taking on the Germans alone. But France, as it happened, was in the midst of a wrenching election campaign, not a propitious moment for a military venture. That venture, moreover, as France's commanding generals made clear, would not be a minor one. The nation had no plans for a partial mobilization, so it was all or nothing. Into the bargain, the Chief of the General Staff, Maurice Gamelin, counseled caution. The Germans were well prepared as he saw it (Gamelin overestimated German strength) and the French were not. The remilitarization of the Rhineland in the end went unopposed.[8]

The events of 1935–6 left French diplomacy in a shambles. They were "the wrecking of French foreign policy," in William Shirer's vivid phrasing.[9] Germany had always harbored revisionist ambitions in the East, but now, as Hitler's Rhineland gambit made all too clear, it had its sights set on overturning the Versailles order in the West as well. France stood in imminent danger, and it had few partners it could count on. The regional alliances in the East remained in place, but that was about it. The prospects of an entente with Italy had collapsed, killed off by fascist power-grabbing in Ethiopia and Spain. Belgium and Britain, in pursuit of unilateral advantage, had turned their backs, and international institutions had proven themselves useless. Briandism was dead. It was an estimable package of policies but ill adapted to deal with a Hitler, and that was plain enough by mid-decade.

French policy-makers, however, were not at a complete loss. They maintained appearances in the East, preserving treaty ties to Poland and Czechoslovakia and keeping the option of a Soviet alliance open, and now efforts were redoubled to persuade Britain to abandon its splendid isolation and commit itself to keeping the peace on the continent by military means if necessary. This choice for Britain was as fateful as it was puzzling: fateful because anti-communist British policy-makers would in due course put a damper on France's already tentative efforts to cultivate the Soviet Union as an ally, and puzzling because Britain made no secret of its reluctance to get involved in continental affairs, a reluctance already in evidence in its hands-off conduct at the time of the Rhineland crisis.

Yet the British option was not in fact as mysterious as all that. Memories from Great War days of the *entente cordiale* had not yet faded, and Britain was, like France itself, a democracy, an ideological kinship that carried all the greater weight in a Europe more and more dominated by dictatorships. Not least of all, for all its obvious hesitations to get involved on the continent, Britain was not immovable on the issue. In the aftermath of the Rhineland setback, the British agreed to send two divisions to France in case of an unprovoked German attack (provided, of course, that the British government at that time still judged the gesture worthwhile).[10]

This was something, albeit not much, and for the moment, that was as far as the British were prepared to go. At the outbreak of the Spanish Civil War in July 1936, the Blum government made known to London policy-makers its intention to help the Spanish Republic; the British made it just as clear that they would not back up the French should intervention escalate into something more serious. It was at this juncture that Blum abandoned his initial, interventionist impulse to pursue instead an international non-intervention pact. Yet, still the British continued to hold back. Neville Chamberlain became prime minister in the spring of 1937, and in the following months the new government made clear that it had no more interest in preserving Czechoslovakia's territorial integrity than the outgoing Baldwin administration. Nor were the British above meddling in French affairs to advance the careers of appeasement-minded politicians to their liking. Blum left office in the summer of 1937 and then made a brief one-month comeback the following March. He appointed to the Ministry of Foreign Affairs Joseph Paul-Boncour, an advocate of a firm policy vis-à-vis the Germans. But then Blum's majority collapsed, and Blum himself was succeeded as prime minister by

Edouard Daladier. The British embassy in Paris agitated to block Paul-Boncour's reappointment. London wanted the Ministry of Foreign Affairs to go to the more temporizing Camille Chautemps. In one sense, Britain did not get its way: the job went to Georges Bonnet. In another it did, for Bonnet turned out to be a hard-core appeaser.[11]

France needed an ally and set its sights on Britain, but the response was half-hearted at best. The British were not so much bossy, which the "governess" metaphor might suggest, as they were reticent and hard to pin down. British attitudes, however, began to unfreeze in the wake of the Munich fiasco.

How disastrous the Munich crisis was for French diplomacy is all too clear. Hitler bullied Czechoslovakia, a French ally, into handing over the Sudetenland, a chunk of borderland territory essential to Czechoslovakia's defense. The French, following Britain's lead, acquiesced to Nazi terms at the Munich conference in September 1938. This is a story of sell-out, no doubt, so why did the French go along?

It was Hitler's annexation of Austria in March 1938, the so-called Anschluss, that first stoked French fears about German intentions vis-à-vis Czechoslovakia. French policy-makers worried, and with good cause, that Czechoslovakia might be next on Hitler's list and invited the British to issue a joint declaration guaranteeing Czech territorial integrity. The British demurred, and the British Foreign Secretary, Lord Halifax, explained why: "Quite frankly, the moment is unfavorable, and our plans, both for offence and defense, are not sufficiently advanced."[12] In the weeks following, much as the French had anticipated, Hitler began to beat the drums about the Czech borderlands. Daladier traveled to London in April to try to induce the British to make common cause against the German threat, laying out in the plainest terms what he thought was at stake. Hitler did not just seek territorial advantage in Czechoslovakia, but far, far more: "the domination of the Continent in comparison with which the ambitions of Napoleon were feeble." The British remained unpersuaded. Chamberlain didn't think the "picture was really so black." Hitler didn't want to destroy Czechoslovakia and, even if he did, there was no way to prevent him from doing so.[13]

And so France, as in March 1936, faced the prospect of war against Germany without back-up from a great-power ally (though the Czechs, with an army of thirty-five divisions, were far from a negligible partner). Daladier hesitated. He was not certain public opinion was ready for all-out war, and France's military chiefs were discouraging. The Luftwaffe, the French premier was told, outclassed France's air arm by a wide margin. The British favored a negotiated settlement. Perhaps then it was best, given the unfavorable circumstances, to let the British take the lead.[14]

Yet however profound the setback, Munich did advance the cause of Franco-British rapprochement, and from the French point of view this was compensation of a sort. Daladier grasped the extent of the defeat and took steps to right the situation. He was not an appeaser in the way Chamberlain was. Chamberlain believed that Munich would bring, as he put it, "peace for our time," but Daladier had no such illusions. As he flew back to Paris from Munich, he expected the crowds waiting at Le Bourget airport to be enraged—Munich had been a failure after all—but they were in a cheering mood instead, prompting Daladier to a derisive snort: "Ah, les cons [the fools]," he is supposed to have exclaimed. He understood that Munich did not mean an end to the German menace, and the French took positive steps to get themselves ready for any future showdown. In December 1938, Daladier sent a delegation to the United States to purchase up to a thousand aircraft. Munich had got Roosevelt's attention, and the US president was disposed to work with the French.[15] Nor did the French play such a passive role as all that during the Munich crisis itself. They persuaded Britain to make a double promise: to guarantee the borders of the Czechoslovak rump and to side with France in case of a war with Germany, and plans were made to back up such commitments. The British and French militaries entered into staff talks in January 1939. Britain added Holland

and Switzerland to the list of continental countries it was pledged to defend. And soon there was discussion of expanding Britain's continental commitment in the event of war from a meager two divisions to an army several times that size. It's not that Chamberlain had given up on hopes of appeasing Hitler but that British public opinion had begun to harden against the Nazis, creating pressure on British policy-makers to get tougher. The policy-making establishment itself, moreover, was growing anxious that it was the French who might now be getting cold feet and so felt some inclination to make gestures toward deepening an alliance about which it had once harbored so many second thoughts.[16]

Munich then at last got the French what they wanted: a serious continental commitment from the British. There was an added bonus in America's apparent willingness to mobilize its productive capacity on France's behalf. Hitler's decision to take over all of Czechoslovakia in mid-March 1939—the Prague coup—solidified the new line-up. Another round of Anglo-French staff talks beginning in May resulted in an agreement as to how the two powers planned to coordinate military efforts in the event of war with Germany. More than that, Britain now seemed prepared not just to go along but to take the initiative, promising to guarantee Poland's territorial integrity.[17] The British acted on their own, unbidden by the French. What a contrast with the year preceding, when France had tried but failed to elicit just such a gesture in defense of a beleaguered Czechoslovakia. The diplomatic stage was set for war, and Hitler put the machinery in motion. He threatened Poland in the summer of 1939, which in turn activated French and British commitments. To be sure, there was lingering hope that war might yet be averted by a last-minute deal. Mussolini proposed calling an international conference to hash out some kind of settlement, a Munich conference redux. The British didn't bite, however (though Chamberlain was tempted), and neither did the French. When the matter was brought up in a cabinet meeting by Foreign Minister Bonnet, who was well disposed to the idea of another conference, Daladier, "bristling with anger and contempt, turned his back."[18] Hitler wanted a fight, and this time Britain and France were ready to oblige.

Yet one important piece to the story is still missing. France in 1935–6 turned to Britain as its best hope, but the British reaction was foot-dragging. Why didn't France at this juncture go all out in pursuit of a Soviet alliance? The Soviets themselves were willing. Stalin was at the time encouraging Communist Parties across Europe to enter into Popular Front alliances while, at the diplomatic level, negotiating with potential anti-fascist partners. Well, it's not as though the French cold-shouldered the Soviets outright. In the summer of 1939, the two powers (along with Britain) entered into substantive talks to coordinate military planning vis-à-vis the Germans, but there were always anti-communist elements in the French establishment, civil and military, which were opposed to any formal alliance. It was fine to go through the motions of negotiation—this might deter Hitler—but it was another matter to clinch the deal.[19]

But even had the French shown more follow-through, it's not at all clear that the Soviet alliance was a workable option. The British were against it and said as much.[20] They were opposed in part because of deep-seated suspicions of communist intentions but also because they doubted the military value of the Red Army. Stalin had conducted a massive and none too secret purge of senior officers in 1937–8, expelling or executing outright thousands, leaving the institution stripped of its most experienced commanders. What value was there working with such a partner? From the French point of view, a military pact with the Soviet Union would alienate Britain and might not bring much military advantage.

Not just that: Poland was a problem. The Poles did not get on with the Czechs, and hated the Soviets. When Hitler gobbled up the Sudetenland in the wake of the Munich crisis, Poland profited from the occasion and snatched a piece of Czech territory for itself—Těšina (Teschen in German). In the months following, as we have seen, France and Britain engaged in intensive military talks with the Soviet Union. But for show to become reality, provision had to be made for the transit of the Red Army through either Romanian or Polish territory, and this the Poles would not tolerate under any circumstances.[21] They did not trust the Soviet Union, and it is well worth pondering whether the Soviet Union was in fact trustworthy. Consider, for example, the impact of Soviet intervention in Spain during the Civil War. The USSR alone among foreign powers came to the aid of the Spanish Republic, but aid also afforded the Soviets leverage. They did not take as much advantage of it as is sometimes supposed, but their outsized presence on the scene empowered local communists who engineered a quasi-takeover of the republican cause, and woe to non-communist loyalists who got in the way. The Poles no doubt feared that a similar fate awaited them. Lord Halifax understood all too well why Poland had balked at the prospect of welcoming Soviet forces onto Polish territory. "An intelligent rabbit," he later wrote, "would hardly be expected to welcome the protection of an animal ten times its size, whom it credited with the habits of a boa constrictor."[22] Neither Polish policy-makers nor Halifax were that far wrong in their assessment of what the Soviet Union was capable of. In August 1939 the USSR abandoned its diplomatic efforts to build an anti-fascist front and elected instead to negotiate a non-aggression pact with the Nazis. Stalin and Hitler agreed to carve up Poland between them, and the Soviets got Finland, Estonia, Latvia and a piece of Romania into the bargain. Why the Soviets entered into the deal will be discussed in a moment. The point, though, is that it was not unreasonable on the part of the Poles—or of the French for that matter—to suspect Soviet motives.

There is much to criticize in the conduct of French diplomacy in the 1930s. Forceful action at the time of the Rhineland and Czech crises would have stopped Hitler, but the French did not take it. All the same, France's diplomatic record was not entirely dismal. The battering of events prompted policy-makers to rethink the Briandist commitments of the 1920s. By 1935 or 1936 at the latest France had shed its illusions about the effectiveness of collective security and begun casting about for military allies to face down the Nazis. There were flirtations with Italy and the Soviet Union, but in the end Britain was fixed upon (rightly, as it turned out) as the most promising partner. The British made small gestures of reciprocation, enough to keep the French interested, but did not get serious until after Munich. The alliance gained momentum thereafter, especially in the wake of the entry of German troops into Prague in March 1939. It was in due course buttressed by material assistance from the United States, such that when Hitler next threatened—over Poland—the Allies, as they may now be called, were ready to step up.

The French may be reproached for not having acted with greater urgency, but then again, if the French were slow-moving, what about the British and the Americans? The French may be reproached for not pursuing the Italian and Soviet options with more determination, but then again, were Mussolini and Stalin, both of whom ended up as territory-grabbing cronies of the Nazis, such reliable prospects? They weren't, of course, and it is a hard thing to scold France for hewing to its Anglo-American friends rather than supping with dictators.

And in any event, it is well worth asking who in the 1930s boasted a foreign policy more far-sighted and effective than that of France. Not the Belgians and Dutch, to be sure, who hunkered down in an ostrich-like neutralism. The case of Great Britain is more complicated. It was a vast, imperial power with interests in the Mediterranean and Far East. In the era of the Great Depression, Britain's resources were stretched and what it wanted most was a quiet continent, not one divided into quarreling blocs. In the 1920s the French might well have seemed the most troublesome cross-Channel power, so inflexible were they when it came to the application of the Versailles Treaty. Hitler's rise made France look less unreasonable, but the British went on believing that the best course lay in calming tensions down. Hence appeasement, which made eminent sense to a power that felt its real interests lay outside of Europe. Munich, followed by the German march into Prague, compelled a major reassessment, however, and now the French alliance began to seem like a more attractive proposition. All the same, British policymakers remained reluctant to engage troops on the continent; they meant to commit as small a force as possible, leaving it up to the French to handle the Wehrmacht almost by themselves. Chamberlain, moreover, remained at the helm of British policy, and, though infuriated by German duplicity at Munich, he continued to be an appeaser at heart. It is understandable why British policymakers, so empire-centered, took such a long time to grasp fully what was happening on the continent. Britain, moreover, sobered by memories of the Great War, was bound to think many times over before sending armies of any substantial size to France's side. Whatever the explanation, the point is this: Britain was slower than France to take the measure of the Nazis, and even when it did, it still hesitated to commit ground forces in large numbers.[23] The country was able to imagine engaging itself in a war of "limited liability"—a concept dear to the military strategist Basil Liddell Hart—but no more.

What is true of the British is true a fortiori of the Americans. It is not quite right to label US policy in the

1930s as isolationist. Policy-makers looked on the Western hemisphere as America's backyard, a sometime unruly neighborhood that required periodic pruning and care. The United States had interests in the Pacific as well. Hawaii was US territory, the Philippines a dependency, and China a friend of long standing, all of which prompted policy-makers to react with alarm to Japanese encroachments in the region. Even in its relations with Europe, the US was not altogether hands-off. To be sure, rising tensions on the continent moved Congress in 1935 to pass the first Neutrality Act, banning the sale of arms to any and all belligerents in the event of war. The legislation was renewed and revised several times in the years following. The 1937 version, however, included a clause authorizing the sale of non-military supplies to buyers on a cash-and-carry basis, a provision helpful to well-heeled powers such as Great Britain.[24]

What the United States did not want, however, were extra-hemispheric military complications. America was not ready to take the Japanese on head to head, and the thought of sending troops to Europe remained anathema. The Great War had soured the United States on direct intervention in European affairs, and even Munich, which changed much in US thinking, did not change this. Roosevelt began to frame hemispheric defense in more expansive terms, necessitating an American naval and air build-up that would persuade potential enemies to keep at a safe distance. The president, moreover, was more and more determined to facilitate French and British rearmament, finding ways to enable the French in particular to tap into America's stepped-up arms production. Once the war got under way, of course, America's oft-proclaimed "neutralism" remained an obstacle to such deals, but Roosevelt managed to finesse the problem by redefining neutrality. Yet one more Neutrality Act was passed in November 1939, but this time the bill featured a cash-and-carry provision that sanctioned the sale, not just of non-military materiel, but of arms as well. Jean Monnet, the French statesman and future Father of Europe, dubbed the United States the "arsenal of democracy," a flattering sobriquet. Yet arms provision was as far as America was prepared to go. No American Expeditionary Force was contemplated. In June 1940 a France on the verge of defeat came pleading to the United States for a military boost. Roosevelt, though sympathetic, still answered with a firm no. America was not as isolationist as is sometimes thought; under the president's constant prodding, its "neutralism" took on a more and more pro-British and pro-French slant. Nevertheless, America was several steps behind the British, not to mention the French, in catching on to the true nature of the Nazi threat. As for what to do about it, the US, up to the outbreak of the war in Europe and beyond, never imagined it would have to do

easy destruction of the once-powerful German Communist Party prompted the Soviets to reconsider. The Germans now seemed the most immediate threat, and a policy of seeking out anti-fascist alliances the most promising avenue of self-protection. But then how did the Soviet Union's putative anti-fascist partners, Britain and France, end up conducting themselves? They bargained with the Soviet Union but would not close the deal, all the while treating the Germans with an appeasing prudence. Stalin knew that capitalism meant war. The British and French had meddled in Russian affairs, and now there was Nazi Germany, which missed no chance to saber-rattle and threaten. A conflagration was coming, and Stalin did not want the Soviet Union to be the first target of attack. Yet, as he came to see it, that is just what Britain and France intended. To be sure, they talked with the Soviets about a deal but always found one obstacle or another to clinching the bargain, and all the while they went on conciliating the Germans. What was Stalin to conclude but that the French and British weren't serious about an anti-fascist coalition and harbored unstated hopes that Nazi aggression would turn eastward toward the Soviets. In the summer months of 1939, even as negotiations with France and Britain bumped along, Stalin prepared an about-face, entering into secret talks with Hitler's emissaries. The result was the Nazi-Soviet pact, announced in August, which struck the European diplomatic scene like a thunderbolt.[26]

The pact was, from Stalin's point of view, a stroke of genius. The imperialist powers would still fight but now among themselves. In the event that Germany emerged victorious, Stalin did not doubt it would attack the Soviet Union next, but the Germans would by then be exhausted and much less dangerous, and the Soviets would have rearmed in the meantime. One more thing: the Nazi-Soviet pact, as we have seen, defined spheres of influence, assigning a large swath of Eastern Europe to Soviet control. In an addendum to the pact, the Germans acknowledged a Soviet interest in Lithuania as well. In short order, Stalin translated "sphere of influence" into military occupation, marching into eastern Poland in September 1939. Things did not go so well in Finland. The Soviet dictator first attempted to blackmail the Finns into territorial concessions, but they refused to cooperate. Stalin then launched an invasion in November, which ran into difficulties. In the end, the Soviets got all the territory they wanted and more, but the adventure had been a good deal more costly than anticipated. The setback, however, did not dissuade Stalin from striking again in mid-1940, annexing the three Baltic states and browbeating Romania into yielding Bessarabia. The Soviet Union's borderlands were now that much deeper. This might not deter a

German attack, but it would reduce the Germans' chance of success.

France's defeat up-ended all Stalin's calculations. He had the territorial buffer he desired, but the Germans were not exhausted. The Soviet Union needed to accelerate its rearmament program, and so, much like France at Munich, it bought time by appeasing. The Germans moved into Yugoslavia on 6 April 1941. The Soviet Union had signed a non-aggression pact with the Yugoslav government earlier that very day but, nonetheless, took no action. That is not in fact quite right: the Soviets did do something, but what they did was intended to placate Germany and its friends. The Soviet Union signed a neutrality pact with Japan in April 1941 and in May extended recognition to the anti-British regime in Iraq.[27] None of this, of course, slowed German preparations for an invasion. Stalin's generals took note of the concentration of German forces on the Soviet border and requested that the Red Army be put on full alert. Stalin refused, fearing the Germans might interpret the move as a provocation—this in June 1941 on the very eve of Operation Barbarossa.[28]

Neutralists and appeasers, France among them, abounded in the 1930s. France was among the first, however, to begin looking for alternatives to appeasement, taking "the lead," as Peter Jackson has put it, "in diplomatic attempts to build an anti-German front in Europe."[29] The front cobbled together, however, did not include the Soviet Union. Western anti-communism explains Soviet isolation but only in part: the Soviets themselves did not trust the imperialist powers, opting instead for a "sphere of influence" bargain with Germany that proved to be catastrophic, leaving them just as vulnerable, if not more so, to the German war machine as the Western Allies.

No one got it right when it came to facing down Hitler, but France's record was not as dismal as often portrayed. It was the first among Western powers to jettison appeasement, and in the aftermath of Munich, it succeeded in coaxing a reluctant Great Britain into an anti-German alliance. Poland remained a friend, and there was hope Belgium and Holland might come around too in the event of actual war. The Soviets, of course, were never welcomed into the anti-German fold as full-fledged partners, and the reasons why have been catalogued. That may well have been a mistake, but it is an understandable one. As for the Soviets themselves, they made a high-stakes bet in August 1939 when they broke off talks with France and Britain to enter into a pact with Hitler. That wager turned out to be a losing one. French diplomacy does not deserve kudos for prescience or imagination, but French policy-makers did well enough in trying circumstances—and who, for that matter, did any better?

CHAPTER 2

ARMAMENTS AND MORALE

It was France, however, that was knocked out of the war, not Great Britain, the United States, or the Soviet Union. Pétain's lament about a paucity of allies was too quick: France had partners enough. One more in the shape of the Soviet Union would no doubt have made a significant, even decisive difference (not that Pétain himself would have favored such a course), but this was not, as we have seen, a viable option. The more desperate circumstances post-Operation Barbarossa would reweight the calculations of Western policy-makers not yet swept away by Hitler's armies, but their number by then no longer included the French.

Yet if Pétain was wide of the mark on the matter of allies, perhaps he got it right when it came to military preparedness and the state of national morale. Fears of German military superiority and doubts about the steadiness of public opinion did indeed cause French statesmen to falter in both 1936 and 1938. Do not such fears and doubts demonstrate that all was not in order in the house of France? Recent work on the subject suggests a less doleful conclusion. In fact, on the matter of rearmament, there is now building consensus that the French effort was nothing short of "extraordinary."[1] Once again, moreover, it is worth asking who got it right anyhow. Were other nations that much better prepared than the French to take on the Nazis?

There's no denying that the French military was in a sorry state in the mid-1930s. In 1928 military service had been cut to one year, resulting in a general reduction in the number of men under arms at any one time. France's army was no more than half a million strong in 1930, and the professional core was a good deal smaller than that, not much larger in fact than the truncated army permitted the Germans under the terms of the Versailles Treaty. Professionals did not so much constitute a combat-ready fighting force as a training cadre tasked with turning green conscripts into something like soldiers in the short time period permitted. Factor in the shrunken state of investment in arms production, the consequence of Depression-era budget cutting, and the picture grows darker still. France's army in the mid-1930s was under-manned, ill trained, and short on modern weaponry.[2] None of this would have mattered so much were it not for Nazi Germany, which had made rearmament a top priority, boosting the portion of the national income set aside for military spending from just under 1 percent in 1933 to 10 percent in 1935.[3]

France did not turn a blind eye to what was happening across the Rhine. In 1935 the term of military service was doubled from one year to two, and with the coming of the Blum government, the pace of arms spending picked up. There is more than a little irony in this. Vichy wanted to blame the defeat of 1940 on a lack of preparedness and battened on Léon Blum as the culprit-in-chief. The regime mounted a show trial in Riom, central France, in 1942 to make its case. There is no doubt that Blum, a socialist of deep convictions, had no truck with militarism and held war in horror. Yet he held Nazism in greater horror, and under Blum's administration 14 billion francs were poured into weapons manufacture. As one historian has put it: ". . . when it came to public expenditure, the Popular Front did more for guns than for butter."[4] Blum oversaw the semi-nationalization of the aircraft industry. The move was designed to rationalize a sector fragmented among numerous small firms, concentrating productive capacity that in turn would facilitate aircraft manufacture on a mass scale.[5] The reorganization proved disruptive at first but began to pay dividends in 1938–9. The Daladier administration that took office in the spring of 1938 ratcheted up arms production, and it was the weaponry of modern warfare—tanks and airplanes—that got the most attention.[6] On the eve of war, the French army had achieved rough numerical equality to the Germans in armor.[7] France's air force was still smaller than the Luftwaffe, but the situation was not altogether bleak. French aircraft production was accelerating at a rate the Nazis could not match, and by early 1940, France and Britain together were churning out a higher total of warplanes than Germany.[8] In 1938, France's air arm was not yet a match for the Reich's, but it was on course to becoming so by 1941.[9] In the meantime, purchased US aircraft made up part of the difference, not to mention the Royal Air Force, which was a formidable force in its own right spearheaded by the redoubtable Spitfire fighter plane.

It is worth underlining in this connection how rapid and massive the French military build-up was. France's military budget skyrocketed from 12.8 billion francs in 1935 to 93.7 billion francs in 1939. The nation was investing 2.6 times as much on armaments production on the eve of the Second World War as it had on the eve of the First.[10] The quality of France's new weaponry, moreover, was on the whole respectable, if not first rate. The

Morane interceptor lacked the speed of the Messerschmitt 109, but when it came to fighter planes France's Dewoitine 520 was said to be superior to any of its German counterparts. There was no better medium tank in the world than France's SOMUA. The heavier Char B was a yet more formidable machine, but its small fuel capacity limited its range of action, and French tanks in general did not come equipped with effective radio communications.[11] Not least of all, France's late-decade armaments boom had a major side benefit: it helped bring an effective end to the Depression. Unemployment, the textile sector apart, all but disappeared. Daladier's May 1938 devaluation and his disciplinary labor policies—in November he gutted Popular Front legislation limiting the work week to forty hours—boosted investor confidence. Capital that had fled France came flooding back, a morale booster for policy-makers who now had the cash resources to finance a war over the long haul.[12]

But perhaps this scenario is too up-beat. It may be that France did a lot to rearm, but didn't the effort come too late? It was catching up to the Germans, but the French still were not a match for them in 1940. And in any event, it's been argued, when measured against Britain's own build-up, France's looks a lot less impressive, even a failure—so there's a lot less room for congratulation than I have allowed.[13]

The problem with the "too late" argument is its focus on France in isolation. The French by themselves were not and would never have been Germany's military equal. The French, however, did not fight alone, and so the issue needs to be restated: Was Germany better equipped for war in May 1940 than France and its allies? The answer to this question is a qualified no. Once war was declared, the Belgians and Dutch abandoned neutralism and at last aligned with Britain and France. Together, the four powers fielded more divisions than the Germans. France by itself had almost as many tanks as the Wehrmacht, but France was not by itself: it was reinforced by a British ally with a tank force of its own, however modest in size. As for airpower, the Luftwaffe outstripped France's air force by a wide, albeit shrinking, margin, but not the combined air fleets of France and Britain together. Numbers, of course, do not tell the whole story. French tanks were impressive war engines, but they had design flaws, and a lot would depend on how they were used. France's warplanes were outclassed by Germany's, but the British had a fighter fleet second to none, as the Battle of Britain would in due course demonstrate. Once again, much would depend on how the Allies exploited the weaponry at their command. The Germans, then, may have enjoyed a qualitative edge in armaments, but that edge was not so great as to be decisive in itself. What mattered was deployment. This was a question not of rearmament policy but of tactical doctrine, a separate (though not unrelated) set of issues that will be taken up presently. For the moment, it's clear that the combined Allied rearmament effort, as of 1939–40, was at least satisfactory and that France's contribution in men and tanks was far greater than anyone else's.

The Allies had caught up to the Germans, but more than that: in a year or two, Allied productive capacity, now running full throttle, threatened to swamp Germany's own war effort hands down. The German high command was aware of this and did not relish the prospect of war. The Führer, however, wanted a fight, convinced that aggression was the surest path to getting his way. He had courted war over Czechoslovakia and was disappointed when it didn't come, and he was ready to do so again at the earliest opportunity. German war planners acceded to the Führer's will and, if there was to be war, judged it better to take the gamble now before the Allies grew too strong. Even then, a war-hungry Hitler had to bear down on his underlings to get them to accelerate their preparations.

It may be that the Allies were ready enough to fight in 1939. The accusation still stands, though, that France did not do as good a job getting ready for war as Great Britain. But why fix on Britain as the standard of success? Why not include the Soviet Union, the United States, or even Germany itself in the discussion?

The Soviets did not have much to boast about. Stalin, as we have seen, subjected the Red Army to a thoroughgoing purge in 1937–8. The resultant disarray explains in part the Soviet Union's poor performance in the Russo-Finnish War of 1939–40. And still there was turmoil in the senior ranks: as late as June 1941 a full three-quarters of Red Army officers had been on active service for less than a year.[14] This is not to say that the Soviets did not undertake a massive military build-up. Military spending accounted for roughly 10 percent of the national budget in the early 1930s, a figure that shot up to 25 percent in 1939, and the number of men under arms quadrupled over the same period, skyrocketing from 1 to 4 million.[15] On the weapons front, France's defeat spurred Stalin to speed up tank procurement, a wise decision, though note how late it came. As for the air force, its sorry state had little to commend it. The overall picture, despite important strides, was not an encouraging one, and the Soviet brass knew it. In May 1940, Generals Zhukov and Timoshenko drafted a report on the state of the Soviet armed forces. As one historian summed up the team's findings: "the army on the whole did not display particular vigilance, battle-readiness, steadfastness in defense . . ."[16]

That said, the Soviets were a good deal better prepared for war than the United States. At the time of the Battle of France, the American army had an estimated 245,000 men under arms, making it the twentieth largest in the world, just behind the Dutch. A peacetime draft was instituted some months later, but congressional support was precarious. The measure came up for renewal in August 1941 and passed the House of Representatives by a single vote, this as the Wehrmacht was sweeping across the Soviet Union and Japan's armies were making ever deeper advances into Southeast Asia.[17] But, of course, the United States at this stage had no intention of involving itself in a ground war of any magnitude. American policy-makers understood war preparedness less as a question of manpower than one of hardware. The United States, it was judged, needed ships and planes most, and so that is where the American build-up began. Munich, as we have seen, marked a first turning point, although how great was the change can be overstated. At the outset of the war in Europe, the United States was spending just a meager 1.4 percent of gross national product (GNP) on defense.[18] But then came the fall of France, which had as sobering an effect on US decision-makers as it had on their Soviet counterparts. In the period 1937–40 the American government had ordered a total of eight battleships; in the aftermath of the French defeat, it ordered an additional nine. The enactment of Lend-Lease in March 1941 spurred on the pace. America was now spending over

11 percent of GNP on defense, but an additional point still needs to be made.[19] At the time of Operation Barbarossa, the United States was just beginning to show what its military-industrial complex was capable of, yet for the moment the "cupboard was almost bare." The necessary arms were in production but not ready for use, and America's enemies were conscious of how things stood. The United States, according to Japanese estimates, had almost three times more warship tonnage under construction than Japan did in 1941, and the conclusion that followed from this was a simple one: the US was unready now, but it would not be unready for much longer. The December attack on Pearl Harbor, of course, was the consequence of such calculations, a stinging defeat for the United States.[20] Much as the Franco-British build-up prompted the Nazis to preemptive action, so did the American build-up spur on the Japanese. The United States, it may be ventured, was less prepared for the onslaught it ended up facing than the French and British, but then again, America did not have the Wehrmacht to deal with (not for another few years), and it benefited from the buffer of a vast ocean that kept its adversary beyond striking distance of the US mainland.

On the matter of adversaries, it is well worth considering just how prepared the Germans themselves were. In the pre-war years, the French overestimated German military might time and again and, when defeat came, tended to explain it as the inevitable outcome of an unequal fight. France, a nation of peasants and shop-keepers, was just no match for the German industrial dynamo. Yet Germany had a peasantry of its own, larger in absolute terms than the French peasantry, and it also had a small-business and artisanal sector that was far from negligible. As for German "military might," the Wehrmacht fielded what amounted to two armies in the Second World War, a mechanized, fast-striking force and a much larger and slower-moving one made up of foot soldiers and horses. The massive, multi-million-man army that was hurled against the Soviet Union in June 1941 was composed in one part of the former but in three parts of the latter.[21]

All the same, there is no denying the staggering wallop the Wehrmacht had the capacity to deliver. The German army's punch derived in good measure from Hitler's unre-lenting determination to assemble a military machine with the advanced weaponry and firepower to crush all opponents. In the first two years of the Nazi regime, the share of national income devoted to armaments shot up from 1 to 10 percent, and that percentage was doubled by 1939, a much higher rate of military spending than in either France or Great Britain. The build-up had come at a heavy cost to consumption, to be sure, which threatened to stoke public discontent. Hitler brushed such concerns aside, convinced that he had the means to keep opinion in check: morale-boosting parades of military hardware, a steady diet of diplomatic and military victories, and the promise of more of the same to come. Where grandiosity and saber-rattling failed, moreover, there was always fear.[22] Dampened consumption, foreign policy adventurism, and authoritarian methods: these were essential ingredients of Hitler's rearmament drive, a recipe just not available to the Allied democracies.

But several additional points bear keeping in mind. The German rearmament drive has been characterized as a "punctuated chaos."[23] It was almost derailed by a financial crunch in 1937, which required all the wizardry of Hitler's economics minister, Hjalmar Schacht, to resolve. A second crisis threatened in the summer of 1939. Shortages of raw materials and of manpower had brought the German war machine to a "critical threshold." The Nazi-Soviet pact and the access to Soviet resources it opened up gave promise of future relief. At the same time, however, the British and French armaments industries had kicked into high gear, seconded by the United States. Germany was working harder than its enemies just to stay a half-step ahead, if that. Finally, well armed as the Germans were, this did not make them invincible. The Polish campaign of 1939 was an undoubted victory, but the victory was won against a much smaller opponent, and the Soviet Union had helped out by launching its own invasion of Poland. Even so, the Reich got a bruising in the fight. A full quarter of the Wehrmacht's tank force had been destroyed or knocked out.[24] Germany's military commanders did not look forward to the prospect of a battlefield confrontation with France, and for good reason.

Looking eastward, France's rearmament push does not appear such a dismal failure. Still, maybe compared to Britain's it was. On one level, the issue is a false one. If France possessed an ally that was yet more productive in arms than it was, this was welcome news, just as it was welcome news for Britain (and not a token of its short-comings) that the United States, the most dynamic arms manufacturer of them all, stood by its side in the aftermath of the French defeat. Having well-equipped allies is a plus. Nonetheless, it is fair to ask whether Britain was making a disproportionate contribution to the common arms effort. This would be proof of a sort that a France in decline was incapable of keeping up its side of the bargain. Britain got into the business of rearming later than France, and even then, the British remained skittish about committing ground forces to the continent, a reluctance that did not evaporate until after the Prague coup in March 1939.[25] The escalating international crisis at last prompted Britain to impose a limited draft in April and then general conscription five months later, a break-through measure by British, albeit not French, standards. Universal military service had been the rule in France since the early years of the Third Republic.

That Britain was a latecomer to the mobilization against Hitler does not mean that in the end it did not do an effective job rearming. There were recriminations in Britain, as in France, after the disaster of 1940. The British Expeditionary Force had come close to total destruction, and the hunt was on for the "guilty men" responsible, with the Treasury identified as the prime suspect. Its stinginess was said to have throttled British rearmament, the poor quality of British equipment in turn accounting for the BEF's near catastrophe. Historians have set the record straight. By 1939, Britain was in fact matching the Germans weapon for weapon in tank and aircraft production.[26]

From here, though, the argument has sometimes been taken a step further to suggest that the British path to rearmament was superior to the French. The British effort, it is said, was more sensitive to trade union interests, and it was better organized.[27] There is something to be said for the first point. Daladier took on and defeated organized labor in November 1938, in contrast to Britain's Tory governments which, once they got serious about rearmament, made an effort to work in collaboration with the trade unions. On the other hand, solicitousness toward organized labor, while good news for social harmony, is not the sine qua non of productivity. The Nazis and Soviets managed to rearm without benefit of independent trade unions. As for France itself, 1938 was indeed a setback for organized labor but not for the nation's arms drive, which heated up in the months following. Workers may have grumbled, but they did not strike, and there was little industrial sabotage.[28] On the matter of organization, Britain had learned a useful lesson from the Great War: the sooner munitions production was rationalized the better. In August 1939, before the next war had even begun, British authorities set up a Ministry of Supply. But France did much the same in October, a mere two months later, and the man placed in charge, Raoul Dautry, was a senior civil servant of exceptional organizational abilities. It is just not clear how much of an advantage, if any, the British enjoyed in this regard. Even conceding that Britain had an edge vis-à-vis the French in arms production circa 1939, the difference was a matter of degree, not of kind. It does not mean that France was failing, just that an ally was having success, a cause not for invidious comparisons but for rejoicing.

What is striking is how taken aback the world was by France's sudden defeat. The Panzer commander Heinz Guderian, as we have seen, described it in miraculous terms. The United States reacted by redoubling its own rearmament effort, Stalin by scrambling to appease a Germany now roaring at its gates. No one, however, was more crushed by the catastrophe than the French people themselves. Propagandists had promised them victory: "We will prevail because we're the strongest," as the slogan went. But had the French public ever believed in the war effort in the first place?

The question of public morale is not easy to evaluate. Pétain, of course, knew no such hesitations. He believed he had an intuitive grasp of the national psyche and did not like what he saw when he looked into France's soul. Too much self-gratification had weakened the nation's martial fiber. Defeat was the near inevitable result and the sole remedy a regime of national atonement and regeneration. To General Maxime Weygand, commander-in-chief at the moment of France's final collapse, the problem was pacifism. The nation's left-wing school-teachers had propagandized against military virtues for twenty years, forming an entire generation too weak-willed to shoulder the burden of France's defense. Historians, of course, eschew such expressions of reactionary penitentialism, but they do make use of words such as pacifism and malaise, "national identity crisis," and decadence to characterize the French state of mind in the years preceding the war.[29]

These are exaggerations. No doubt, the national mood had darkened in the 1930s. France saw itself as "a land of asylum," willing to welcome Europe's tired and hungry, provided they in turn were willing to embrace French ways. Indeed, no country in interwar Europe took in more refugees. A deepening depression in the decade, however, generated a backlash. Laws were passed that made it difficult for the recently naturalized to gain access to "overcrowded" professions such as law and medicine. The influx of refugees fleeing Hitlerian oppression ratcheted up the xenophobic mood. Moviemakers complained about a Semitic invasion that stole jobs from the native-born. The director Marcel L'Herbier pinpointed Blum's accession to power in 1936 as a turning point. That was the moment when "Jewish immigrants" had taken over the movie industry, "remaking it in their image which is assuredly not our own."[30] Then came the Spanish Civil War. Defeated loyalists poured into France late in the decade, prompting heated debates about how to handle them, debates that culminated in the building of a network of internment camps.

Remember, too, how scarred France was by the ravages of the Great War. There were reminders everywhere of what the fighting had cost: monuments to the dead, subway seats reserved for the mutilated, posters and movies recalling the sacrifices made. Veterans' organizations— massive and well organized—preached a message of patriotic pacifism. Such sentiments found loud echoes in parliament among the so-called "*mous*," literally softies, a clique of a hundred or so deputies who favored a prudent, appeasing foreign policy. Nor were the *mous* marginal men. Their number included figures of note and reputation—former Prime Minister Pierre Laval, Camille Chautemps who served a brief stint as premier himself from June 1937 to March 1938, and Georges Bonnet, as of April 1938 and until the outbreak of hostilities France's minister of foreign affairs. The latter two were Radicals, members of France's governing party par excellence, which played a key part in every French administration from 1932 until the war. Waverers and peace-at-any-price appeasers, while a minority, occupied a strategic position in France's political class.

Last of all, there is the question of anti-communism. The participation of the French Communist Party (the PCF) in the Popular Front made it a force to reckon with both in and out of parliament. France's communists were to all appearances steadfast defenders of the anti-fascist line, a commitment that the signing of the Nazi-Soviet pact did not at first alter. PCF deputies voted to finance the war effort in early September 1939. Yet before the month was out, Moscow loyalists in the party had begun to align themselves with Stalin's new policies, repudiating the war as an imperialist exercise. Prime Minister Daladier seized the occasion to dissolve the PCF and arrest forty or so Communist deputies who refused to renounce the party's change of line. Communists, who had labored for much of the 1930s to position themselves as members in good standing of the national community, were now tarred as national pariahs.

Public opinion, on this account, was a cauldron of prejudice: anti-Semitic, defeatist, and anti-communist. It's easy enough to see why the French, so burdened, were unable to mount a concerted war effort and why, once rocked by defeat, they were seduced by the siren calls of Vichy authoritarianism. This picture is not so much false as one-sided, and it is worth querying at the same time whether French opinion, fissured as it was, was so unique in this respect.

The French public did not savor the prospect of hostilities with the Axis powers, but there were clear signs in 1938–9 that it had begun to grasp and to accept that just such a war might be necessary. Mussolini's fascist regime, sensing French weakness post-Munich, did not conceal that it had an eye on France's North African possessions and even on Corsica and the Savoie. Daladier answered back, making clear France's determination to protect its Mediterranean presence, touring Tunisia and Corsica to underscore the point. The French public applauded the prime minister's decisiveness, and its resolve was further stiffened by Hitler's Prague coup. A public opinion poll undertaken in the summer of 1939, one of the first of its kind, asked respondents how France ought to reply in the event Hitler seized the Free City of Danzig, as he had threatened to do. Seventy-six percent of those polled wanted Germany stopped and were prepared to sanction the use of force to that end, as against just 17 percent who preferred peace at any price.[31]

For much of the 1930s, the streets of Paris had been a battleground where left and right fought, sometimes with bare knuckles, for control of public space. There had been right-wing, anti-parliamentary riots in February 1934 that left more than a dozen dead. The left answered back with a series of mass marches that criss-crossed the city in a show of anti-fascist determination. A different, less confrontational climate prevailed in the years just before the war. The crowds turned out in the summer of 1938 to welcome the King and Queen of England, in Paris on a visit. That November marked the twentieth anniversary of the 1918 armistice, and Daladier, who was a veteran of the Great War himself, made sure that the event was commemorated with the appropriate public fanfare. Then in July 1939 began the celebration of the French Revolution's 150th anniversary, marked by a round of well-orchestrated parades and public displays that were still unfolding even as the war broke out. It's hard to tell how deep the new patriotic consensus ran, but one historian has written of the French public's "mood of quiet, guarded optimism" in the face of the looming threat of war, another of its consent to the possibility of armed conflict.[32] What is certain is that once hostilities did break out, no more than a handful of conscripts refused the call to the colors, and in the course of the fighting that ensued there was not a single significant instance of mutiny.

This is not to say that morale ran high, just that France entered the war far less hobbled than is often supposed. Some of the credit for this must go to the prime minister, Edouard Daladier. For a start, he was no René Viviani. Viviani was prime minister when the Great War began. He had made a name for himself in younger days as a socialist lawyer but then had gone on to an unremarkable career in parliament as a fence-sitting pol. If second-rank leadership in a moment of trial is proof of national decomposition, then it was France in 1914, not 1940, that was in trouble. As for Daladier himself, he was, though no Roosevelt or Hitler, a popular figure. He knew how to use the public airwaves, making a favorable impression with listeners who appreciated his down-home, regional accent (he was from the south of France), and distinguished record of military service (he was a combat veteran who had finished the Great War as a captain, having begun it as a private). To be sure, Daladier was not a man of iron will. Munich, when he had bent to the British, proved that. Yet he could give the appearance of taking charge. He had faced down the trade unions and Mussolini and, in September of 1939, seemed ready to take on Hitler. Once the war was under way, Daladier joined in ganging up on anti-war communists, an all too easy mark to be sure, but he also maneuvered to rein in the peace lobby, demoting Bonnet from the Ministry of Foreign Affairs, which he took over himself, to the Ministry of Defense. The defeatists were quieted for the time being, although they continued to plot.

The picture, then, on the eve of the war was a mixed one: France was not rudderless. It had a capable, if not first-class leader, and public opinion stood behind him. The appeasers were not making noises, but they would when the opportunity presented itself. And the depth of the public's commitment to the war effort remained to be tested.

The glass was but half full in France, yet was it that much fuller elsewhere? It was not in the US. In June 1940, at the very moment of France's defeat, 64 percent of the American public opposed entry into the war. Such anti-interventionist sentiment was stoked by the America First Committee, formed that September by students at Yale Law School. The organization, whose membership soon came to number in the hundreds of thousands, lobbied hard to keep public opinion roused against Roosevelt's foreign policy, and the America Firsters were not just a crackpot crew. Yale Law School's student body yielded a pair of first-class recruits in Kingman Brewster, a future Yale president, and Gerald Ford, a future president *tout court*.[33]

In Britain, on the other hand—and it was Britain, apart from France that mattered most—opinion had given up on appeasement by the war's outbreak. The turn had been slow in coming, but it was decisive. Chamberlain, still prime minister when Hitler invaded Poland, might well have orchestrated a second Munich had not the weight of public opinion pressured him to do otherwise.[34] This very fact, though, points to a second, less heartening conclusion: the general public may have come round to recognizing the necessity of war, but not so elements of the British elite who were a good deal cooler about the prospect.[35] In 1933 the Oxford Union had voted by a wide margin a pacifist resolution that "This House will in no circumstances fight for its King and Country." The notorious Cliveden set—an influential coterie of well-born and well-placed appeasers, so named for the home of Lady Nancy Astor where they gathered— was not just anti-war but downright pro-German. Then there was the Conservative Party itself, which (Winston Churchill and a small group of like-minded colleagues apart) hewed to the appeasement line, taking its cue from the appeaser-in-chief Neville Chamberlain. Although he led Britain into conflict, Chamberlain did so with the utmost reluctance, remaining an apostle to the end of cutting a deal with Hitler. It was Chamberlain who said of Czechoslovakia at the time of Munich: "How horrible, fantastic, incredible it is that we should be digging trenches and trying on gas-masks here because of a quarrel in a faraway country between people of whom we know nothing." It was he who, as the Polish crisis began to unfold, did not want to declare war on Germany, and he again, abetted by fellow appeasers in the cabinet, who ran a dithering war effort until May 1940 when, sick and discredited, he was at last brought down in the Commons with the damning oratory of the Conservative MP Leo Amery ringing in his ears: "You have sat too long here for any good you have been doing. Depart, I say, and let us have done with you. In the name of God, go."

The French public had come round to an acceptance of the possibility of war sooner than the British, though not with the same hardened sense of purpose. Political elites were divided in both countries. France's *mous* were a significant, though for the moment chastened, force. In Britain, the appeasers still occupied the high ground of decision-making power when war began, even if their grip had begun to slip under pressure from a belatedly aroused opinion. On the matter of leadership, however, the differences between the two allies were more stark. Daladier was ready to take the fight to Hitler in a way Chamberlain never was. If waffling, appeasing leadership is the sure sign of a nation in crisis, then the decadent power when the war broke out was Great Britain at least as much as France.

The Soviet Union and Germany too for that matter were in no better shape. The Soviet elite, of course, had been purged into submission by a decade of terror, and Stalin was no more merciful to the general public. He feared the USSR's border populations as pools of potential disloyalty. During the years 1936–8, 800,000 non-Russians were deported from the western borderlands to Central Asia. When the Soviets moved into Poland in 1939, 400,000 Poles met a similar fate, as did "several hundred thousand" Balts in 1940.[36] The ever paranoid Stalin did not trust the men he worked with or the minority peoples of the Soviet Union. Hitler, by contrast, boasted a supreme self-confidence, never doubting that he was a man of destiny. The German public, it was reported, did not welcome the prospect of war at the time of the Munich crisis, and as the threat of hostilities loomed once more in 1939, the American newspaper correspondent William Shirer noted the almost visible defeatism on the faces of people in the Berlin streets, but Hitler was not deterred. He was a go-for-broke gambler ready to wager that victory would wash away all trepidations. Such recklessness maddened the Führer's military entourage, however, and in 1938 and again in 1939, staff officers plotted to overthrow him. The chief of the German general staff, Franz Halder, took to carrying a concealed pistol around, intending, should he ever summon the needed courage, to assassinate the Nazi dictator.[37] Nothing came of any of this, but the fact still remains: the Soviet Union and Germany were riven with plots and purges. They were dictatorships that ran roughshod over doubting or unreliable populations with a mixture of bravado and brutality. In comparison, France in 1939 had little to be ashamed of.

Looking from the vantage of September of that year, it is not at all evident that France was bound to lose the war that lay ahead. Its strategic position was not as strong as in 1914: Germany after all did not have to worry in a serious way about a two-front war. Still, France had a redoubtable ally in Great Britain (reinforced as the war got started by belated Belgian and, to a lesser degree, Dutch cooperation). France also had access, in a way it had not in 1914, to American armaments production, which was gathering momentum at a startling pace. In weapons and men, the Allies were a close match for the Germans—more than a match when it came to sea power, less than one when it came to the air. France's finances were sound and its economy, thanks to the military build-up, humming. The politics of the 1930s had been turbulent and polarized, currents of xenophobia and anti-communism running deep in segments of opinion and the political class; but in answer to repeated Axis bullying, there had been a patriotic resurgence. The nation's political leaders may not have been great statesmen, yet they were able enough, skillful and often well-meaning parliamentarians such as democracies are wont to produce. There were nay-saying defeatists, to be sure, but as of 1939 at least, the peace-at-any-price faction had been reduced to backroom maneuvers. France was as ready for war as any of the major belligerents, readier than the US and Soviet Union, at least as ready as Great Britain and Germany.

So why then did France lose and lose in such spectacular fashion? When the war began in earnest, matters of doctrine, battle planning, and on-the-ground operations took center stage. I have argued that France's glass was half full when it came to the matter of war-preparedness. The glass empties out altogether, however, the deeper the military side of the equation is delved into.

PART II

THE BATTLE OF FRANCE

CHAPTER 3

BATTLE PLANS

Marc Bloch was among the first to say it, and the point has now become well-nigh axiomatic: France was still fighting the Great War in 1940, a war of position that placed a premium on defense, concentrated firepower, and entrenched strongholds.[1] There was no greater symbol of such a backward-looking mindset than the Maginot Line, a network of concrete bunkers and fortifications that stretched mile after mile along France's border with Germany from Luxembourg to Switzerland. To Bloch's initial charge has been added a second, just as damning in its way: the determination of France's military planners to make sure that the bulk of the fighting took place elsewhere. This war, unlike that of 1914–18, should not be decided on French soil but in Eastern Europe where

France was content to let the Poles stand or fall alone; or in Belgium where the French planned, once hostilities had got started, to relocate their most battle-ready units. Let others know first-hand the devastations of modern warfare; this time, France meant to spare itself the worst.[2]

The Germans too had learned lessons from the Great War: that the tank was a fearsome weapon and massed armor more fearsome still. The creation of Panzer armies made possible the concentration of striking power, the better to punch a hole in enemy lines and, the hole once punched, to capitalize on the advantage with an unprecedented speed. Add in dive-bombers to demoralize frontline opponents and sow disorder in the enemy's rear, and motorized infantry to consolidate the gains made: the combination made for a new kind of war, conducted at a lightning pace for which the French were just not prepared.

French military strategists hadn't moved with the times, but maybe that was because they were an aging lot. Senior officers in 1939 were on average eight to ten years older than their German counterparts.[3] The issue of motorized attack divisions had in fact come up for debate in the 1930s, with an obstreperous young colonel, Charles de Gaulle, making the case in favor. But he was outmaneuvered (and outranked) by the octogenarian Marshal Pétain who was a firm believer in the supremacy of defensive warfare, a conviction bolstered by his experience as commanding officer at Verdun in 1916.

The received wisdom is hard on the Maginot-mindedness of the French, seen as symptomatic of an officer class (not to say an entire society) grown wary of taking the initiative and out of touch with a fast-paced, mechanized modern world. France was a sitting duck, and to make matters worse, far worse, Hitler struck at the unfortunate French where they were most vulnerable— through the Ardennes forest. The war began in September 1939. Hitler invaded and conquered Poland, paused to repair or replace damaged equipment, and then turned westward, attacking Holland and Belgium first. France, as its battle plan called for, advanced a substantial portion of its armed forces into Belgium and Holland, while the rest hunkered down behind the Maginot Line. The Ardennes were located at the hinge point in France's defensive front, at the weld linking the Maginot Line and French units positioned on Belgian territory. The area, moreover, was not that well defended and for understandable reasons. This was forestland, hard to penetrate and maneuver in, and there was also a river to cross, the Meuse, all in all not the most propitious terrain for an armored assault. Yet this is where Hitler decided to attack in May 1940, a high-risk move that paid off, catching the French by surprise. The choice was consonant with the go-for-broke temperament that made the Führer so difficult for more run-of-the-mill politicians and generals to deal with.

It may have been bad luck for the French that Hitler attacked where he did in 1940. Yet what followed in the wake of the attack was not bad luck but to all appearances further evidence of France's failings as a nation. French troops panicked in the face of the initial Panzer assault. As German motorized divisions then raced westward, cutting a sickle-shaped path en route to the English Channel, the French proved incapable of moving with sufficient speed and decision to mount an effective counter-attack to contain the enemy drive. The end result was the entrapment of France's armies in Belgium and of the British Expeditionary Force stationed there as well. They would in the end be evacuated from Dunkirk to Britain in late May and early June, with Marc Bloch among the evacuees. It was a phenomenal rescue effort that in common memory has redounded more to Britain's credit than to France's. A total catastrophe was thus averted (it is well worth pondering what Britain would have done had its expeditionary force in fact been destroyed), but that was not saying much. The Germans had routed France's armies in Belgium; the Maginot Line was circumvented; and the nation's heartland now lay exposed to a German advance southward. Frightened civilians, Belgian and French but French in the main, took to the roads. The government abandoned Paris for safer quarters to the south-west, first in the Touraine and then, yet further away, at Bordeaux. The haste was so great that it wasn't possible to pack up everything. Officials at the Ministry of Foreign Affairs burned papers in the Ministry courtyard, creating a plume of smoke visible to alarmed neighborhood residents. The government's precipitous departure spurred on the civilian exodus, which in the end swelled to over 8 million. Here then was a nation in disintegration: its armies crushed, its civilians in flight, and its government on the run.[4]

This is the usual story: it is not wrong, but it is partial. Much, but not all, of what it leaves out makes the French defeat look a good deal less "strange" than Bloch and others who borrowed from him imagined. Let's start with French strategic planning. The Maginot Line seemed like a good idea at the time. It was named after André Maginot, minister of defense in 1928, when the line's construction was begun. France was then scaling back its military apparatus, and the Maginot Line served that purpose well. It cost money to erect for sure, but a frontier defended by fortifications required a smaller manpower investment than a frontier defended by soldiers alone. In the actual fighting of 1940, the Germans never made a full frontal assault on the line but, crashing through the Ardennes, outflanked it from the west before eventually enveloping it. Even then, entrapped French armies put up ferocious resistance. The hopelessness of the situation forced an eventual surrender, but the Maginot Line itself was still standing at the end; not one of its major fortresses was captured in the fighting, and in this sense the line did what it was supposed to do.[5]

Yet, if the Maginot Line wasn't such a bad idea, why not extend it all the way to the English Channel? For a number of reasons. The Ardennes were thought to be impassable, and so there seemed no need for fortified positions in that sector. As for France's northern borders, the terrain there was flat and soft, not suitable for heavy fortifications anchored deep in the soil. The north, moreover, was a major industrial region, home to critical mining and metal-making industries. A pitched battle here, with artillery barrages and bombing runs, would disrupt production, crippling France's war effort in the process. Anyhow, extending the line along the Belgian border would send the wrong message to the Belgians themselves. France needed allies and still wanted to woo Belgium into a military partnership. Insert a concrete barrier between the two nations, and the Belgians would no doubt conclude that they were being left to look after themselves, indeed abandoned.[6]

Such reasoning, sound as it was, still left unresolved the problem of how to defend France's northern frontier, a conundrum complicated by Belgium's proclamation of neutrality in 1936. Belgium, it turns out, was not as neutral as all that, and its military planners remained in secret contact with their French counterparts, plotting together what to do in the event of war. The two powers had a clear enough idea how the fighting was supposed to unfold. If, as expected, Germany invaded Belgium, Belgium's own system of fortifications along the Albert Canal and Dyle River would slow the German advance, allowing the French just enough time, moving at top speed, to reinforce the Belgians. The Belgian and French armies, fighting side by side along a single, continuous front, would thus force the Germans to fight a "methodical battle" on terrain of Belgian and French choosing. The two powers made sure that the terrain in question was prepared, peppering it with bunkers, barricades, and minefields believed sufficient to bring any German assault to a standstill.[7]

The Franco-Belgian plan of battle, like the idea of the Maginot Line itself, was not so misconceived as all that. It presupposed that French troops were ready to make a rapid bolt northward, and indeed they were. France's armies in this sector were fully motorized and ready to move. In fact, French units were more motorized on average than German ones.[8] The French had learned something about mobile warfare after all, a good deal more than used to be thought.

As for the idea of fighting a set-piece battle on prepared ground, it wasn't altogether a bad one. In May 1940 the main German thrust, of course, ran through the Ardennes, but it was decided at the same time to launch a diversionary attack into Belgium through the so-called Gembloux Gap, a swath of flat terrain well suited to mobile warfare and to that extent favorable to the Germans. But the French had anticipated that the Germans might strike somewhere in the vicinity and were ready, calling up armored columns of their own, spearheaded by the fearsome SOMUA tank. In the series of encounters that followed, all France's tactical weaknesses were on display. French tanks formed static battle lines that swift German open-field maneuvers were able to disrupt; the French lacked adequate radio equipment, making it hard for them to communicate and regroup, whereas the better-equipped Germans knew no such difficulties. Yet the outcome of the battle turned out to be a draw and, on some accounts, an outright victory for the French.[9] The German attack at the Gembloux Gap, of course, was not the main push but a feint, which may have made a difference in favor of the French. That said, the outcome gives a hint of what French armies could do when attacked where they expected.

For all the defensive-mindedness of France's initial scheme of battle, French military planners did indeed envision an eventual changeover to offensive operations. The idea was to blunt Germany's opening onslaught, using the breathing room gained to undertake a massive military build-up of the kind the French, British, and American economies working together could sustain, but never the German. Once overwhelming superiority in materiel had been achieved, then would come the moment to go on the attack and to crush the Germans by superior force of arms.

Such was the state of French military thinking at the outbreak of the war. Planners had devised a strategy that made sense for a nation like France, an industrial democracy freighted with all too vivid memories of a previous world war that had cost it, proportionate to its population, more men than any other combatant save Serbia. The Germans, in thrall to a high-rolling Führer, might stake everything on an offensive spearheaded by ideology-fueled elite units, but was such an option available to the French? France's was a republican army under the ultimate command of elected politicians bound to be frugal with French lives. Experience taught that offensive operations risked huge losses. It was more prudent not to ask too much of citizen soldiers just called up; better to hold the line until France's industrial might, seconded by that of Britain and America, came into full play—and then make the decisive strike.[10]

And truth to tell, no one had a better strategy ready to hand. The British had no objection to the French scheme. They were content to contribute a modest expeditionary force to help out on the ground and to play what they believed to be a yet more critical role in the air, dispatching bomber squadrons over the Ruhr to devastate German industrial capacity.[11] Such was the British idea: to stymie Germany on the land and cripple its war machine from above, leaving the enemy vulnerable to a final knock-out blow, all at minimal cost in blood to Britain itself. For the slaughter of the Great War had taught Britain a lesson or two as well: that it was better not to attack the enemy head-on but to hit him on the flanks or in the rear, relying on technology rather than manpower to deliver the most punishing blows. In the event, Britain was lucky not to suffer the fate that befell the French. It was saved by the rescue and evacuation of the BEF remnant at Dunkirk, by an English Channel impenetrable to Panzer attack, and by the RAF that beat off the Luftwaffe, assuring British air superiority over England itself and scotching German plans for an invasion of the home islands as a result. In a sense, though, even France's defeat did not alter by much Britain's overall strategic outlook. The United States, once in the war and under pressure from the Soviets to open a second front, advocated an all-out assault on the continent. The British remained loath to go straight at the Germans, preferring more roundabout maneuvers instead, and for a while they succeeded in coaxing the Americans to go along. The Allies first undertook landings in North Africa and Italy before the American Chief of Staff, General George Marshall, insisted on no further delays in making D-Day happen.[12] There was one thing America's entry into the war did not change, however: Britain's commitment to heavy bombing. On this point, British and American military strategists saw eye to eye, and Britain remained committed as ever to pummeling Germany from the air, so much so that the man in charge of Britain's Bomber Command from 1942, Sir Arthur Harris, earned himself the nickname "Bomber Harris."

By 1942, of course, both the USSR and the United States were in the war. At the outset, neither was at all prepared for what was coming. The Soviets had constructed fortifications along the new frontiers acquired in 1939–40, at the same time ramping up armaments production on a colossal scale. Stalin believed he had adequate breathing room and that the Western powers would keep the Germans busy for the time being. But the unanticipated rapidity of France's defeat made plain that he had less breathing room than he thought. And then war games in January 1941 exposed just how unready for actual combat the Soviet Union's armed forces were. Stalin's confidence faltered. The Soviet Union bristled with weaponry, and the Soviet dictator hoped that this would suffice to deter the Germans. But in the event that it didn't, Stalin bent over backward not to undertake any action Hitler might construe as provocative. Intelligence reports were received that the Germans were contemplating a summer offensive and in June 1941 that German troops were in fact massing on Soviet borders. But even then, despite the urging of his generals, Stalin refused to authorize anything more than a partial mobilization lest the Germans take umbrage.

When the Germans launched Operation Barbarossa on 22 June, the attack confounded Soviet war planners in every way. The Soviets had anticipated a one-front assault, a drive toward Kiev in all likelihood, but the Germans came on three fronts at once, pushing not just toward the south-east but toward Moscow and Leningrad as well. Stalin thought he would have a few weeks to mobilize, but the Germans did not give him the time. Not least of all, Soviet strategists had imagined they would be able to blunt the initial German push and then go on the offensive themselves. Instead, the Germans, reproducing what they had done in France but on a yet grander scale, executed a series of sickle-cut maneuvers, enveloping one Soviet army after another at a terrifying pace. In the first six months of fighting, the Soviets lost two hundred divisions, sustaining a mind-boggling 4 million casualties in the process.[13] The Soviet Union's strategic unpreparedness and the scale of its initial defeats were far greater than those of France. Yet the Soviets in the end held fast, whereas the French did not. A portion of the credit must go to Stalin himself, the keystone of the Soviet system; although he buckled, he did not break. In the end, though, it was geography that mattered most. The Soviet Union was big enough to cede territory to the Germans equivalent to many Frances and yet still retain adequate room and resources to carry on the fight. The English Channel was Britain's Maginot Line, the Russian steppes the Soviet Union's.

America too had natural defenses, vast oceans on either side of it. It is pointless to insist further on the United States' lack of readiness for the war. Roosevelt wanted to back up the French and British, but he never imagined sending actual US troops to the continent, and so no attention was given to the matter until the fall of France created a sense of urgency. In the aftermath of Pearl Harbor, US strategists got down to planning operations for the transport of troops overseas, but it was not until spring of 1942, in secret negotiations with the British, that America settled on an overall strategic design aimed at defeating Germany first before turning to Japan. The problem, of course, was how to bring off such a feat.

Sheltered behind its Atlantic redoubt, the US kicked war production into high gear, churning out trucks, tanks, and jeeps on a scale sufficient to equip not just its own fast-expanding military establishment but the British and Soviet armies as well. Germany did its best to interrupt the transfer of American-made manufactures overseas, mounting a devastating U-boat campaign against Allied shipping, but it lost the Battle of the Atlantic, a fatal defeat that made possible a massive build-up of arms and armies in Britain. The pressure was released first in a series of flanking maneuvers—in Morocco and Sicily—and then in a head-on assault at Normandy. Once Hitler's Atlantic wall was breached, the better-equipped Anglo-Americans wore down the Germans, burying them in an avalanche of tanks and bombs. This was the so-called American way of war: the US during the Second World War in effect reinvented General Grant's grinding strategy against the Confederacy in the American Civil War for twentieth-century purposes.[14] In fact, it was the Soviet military that did most of the grinding, but the point is still a valid one. The Third Reich may well have had the most battle-effective armies in the world,[15] but it was no match in a long war against an Allied coalition that enjoyed over-powering industrial supremacy.

But wait a moment: wasn't just such a long-war strategy France's own in the first place? Once France was so swiftly out of the fight, Great Britain had no evident way forward against Hitler. It had thrown in its strategic lot with France, but now that its ally was on the sidelines, the best the British could do was to hang on, which they did with a stoic heroism. The Soviet Union had geared its own military thinking around offensive operations, but Hitler got the jump on the Soviets and sent them reeling. The US, when it got into the fight, was willing at least for a while to follow Britain's strategic lead, hammering away at Hitler's Fortress Europe from the margins. But by 1942–3 a winning strategy had begun to take shape, premised on the Allies' capacity to pound the German military machine into submission over time. It had been necessary first to stave off defeat before it became possible to imagine a way to victory, and this is just what happened. The English Channel held. The Russian plains cushioned the Soviet Union against Germany's Panzer attacks. And the Atlantic Ocean did the same for the US against Hitler's U-boats.[16] What went wrong for the French was not the consequence of a flawed strategic plan: that plan suited France's capabilities well enough, and no one had a better one. What in fact went wrong was that France's defensive line did not hold.

A closer examination of the events of 1939–40, from the outbreak of the war to the onset of the German invasion, will provide a partial explanation of why this should have been so. Civilian error plays a part in this story, as does France's defensive posture that led to missed opportunities. Far more consequential, however, were last-minute changes in battle plans both on the German side and on the French, changes that hugely strengthened Hitler's hand and just as significantly weakened that of France.

On the matter of civilian error, France's wartime administrations, first Daladier's and then, from March 1940, Paul Reynaud's, have been reproached many times over for their willingness to engage in energy-wasting, diversionary adventures. In the Finnish-Soviet winter war of 1939–40, the French, of course, tilted in Finland's favor. There was talk of taking matters a step further, even to the point of declaring war on the Soviet Union. Failure to act in time to forestall a Soviet victory in fact cost Daladier the premiership. He was succeeded by Reynaud, who did not intend to suffer the same fate. In May 1940, in anticipation of a German attack on Norway, the French mounted a joint preemptive strike with Great Britain, the two powers sending troops to secure the Norwegian port of Narvik.

Neither adventure reflected well on the good judgment of the civilian leadership. It is incredible that the French even considered getting into a war with the Soviets when they were already engaged against the Germans, and so it is well worth wondering why French policy-makers gave themselves over to such misconceived schemes. Was it a sign that Daladier and Reynaud had become unhinged, getting cold feet about the long-war strategy and grasping at ploys that promised, however implausibly, a quick exit from the conflict?[17]

There are reasons to think otherwise. After many months of nerve-rattling inactivity, there was growing public and political pressure on France's civilian leadership to do something, anything. Daladier took aim at the Soviet Union, which played well with anti-communists in parliament (a broad coalition that spanned the usual left/right divide); where anti-communism was concerned he didn't need much prodding anyhow. The objective was in part to interrupt the flow of Soviet military materiel to the Germans, and there were proposals in this connection to bomb the Soviet oilfields in far-distant Baku. The Norwegian expedition was similarly conceived to disrupt German supply lines, although in this case it was the blocking of Swedish iron-ore shipments, not the flow of oil, that was at issue. Both schemes had an economic rationale that meshed with the Allies' wider strategy of squeezing the enemy's productive capacity. The Soviet gambit was the more hare-brained of the two, but of course nothing at all came of it. The Norwegian expedition was given the go-ahead and turned out to be a fiasco.

The French, though, were not alone to blame. Anger against the Soviet Union in 1939–40 swept up the British as well, including, not least of all, Winston Churchill. The failure of the Narvik expedition, which the British were involved in as much as the French, drove Chamberlain from office in May, creating the opportunity for Churchill to take over; but there is an irony here, for Churchill himself had been a major booster of the Norwegian scheme.[18] France's civilian leadership in 1939–40 was no more unhinged than Britain's. In any event, however misguided the Finnish and Norwegian affairs, they weren't decisive. The French lost the war in France, not in Scandinavia.

As for missed opportunities, the most important one was no doubt France's failure to initiate offensive operations at the war's very outset while Germany was engaged against Poland. There is wide agreement that the Reich was vulnerable at this moment. General Halder, the Chief of Staff, himself acknowledged as much, conceding that he lacked adequate means to stop the French had they acted with urgency to occupy the Ruhr.[19] Germany, moreover, continued to remain vulnerable for a period thereafter. The invasion of Poland may have been a walkover, but it was a costly one, immobilizing, as noted, a full quarter of Germany's armored units.[20] Yet the French, ever wedded to the defensive, opted not to seize the initiative.

The consequences of such passivity were unfavorable to the French twice over. France itself settled into a waiting mode. This was the so-called *drôle de guerre*, and it was detrimental to both military and civilian morale. Soldiers, dug in at the front, had too much time on their hands. There were efforts made to keep the troops busy reinforcing positions, but the mix of boredom and nervous anticipation that prevailed ate into the front-line soldier's fighting spirit. Back in Paris, such nervous anticipation translated into political squabbling and intensifying pressures to take action. As we have seen, these resulted in the Finnish and Norwegian blunders, both of which cost France's wartime leadership a damaging loss of prestige. The Germans, in the meantime, did not squander the pause that the *drôle de guerre* afforded but profited from it to reequip and come up with a proper plan of campaign against the French.

It may well be that France could have won the war in September–October 1939. Even to entertain such an idea, of course, is to concede a lot: that French diplomacy, whatever its failings, hadn't set the nation up for certain defeat, that France's rearmament drive was not a matter of too little too late. And while the army was idling during the *drôle de guerre*, France's arms industries were not, in particular where aircraft production was concerned.[21] It isn't then as though nothing useful to the war effort got done.

Most important of all, just because France missed a chance to win in the fall of 1939 did not mean it had to lose in the summer following. No doubt, all the waiting around allowed political differences, which the Polish crisis had for the moment submerged, to bubble up once again. The *mous* grew more assertive, agitating to deflect opinion away from the anti-German effort in favor of an anti-communist war against the Soviet Union. Yet that war never happened, and one historian has even written of a "stiffening of resolve" throughout the civilian sector in the spring of 1940 that turned into a veritable "national awakening" (*sursaut national*) once the actual fighting got started and France itself was under invasion.[22] Last of all, it is true that the Germans in many respects made better use of the reprieve afforded by the *drôle de guerre* than did France, but they almost didn't. Hitler was just as zealous about going on the attack as the French were about waiting on events. He wanted in fact to launch an offensive in November 1939 at a time when the post-Poland refitting of the Wehrmacht was not yet complete; and worse still from the German point of view, the plan of attack at that time had not yet fixed on the Ardennes as the main target but on points further north where the French lay in wait.[23] Had Hitler got his way, the Battle of France might have turned out differently, but the dissuasive efforts of his generals and above all inclement weather put a damper on the Führer's self-destructive impetuosity, allowing time for better-thought-out preparations.

This is just what the Germans did. Over a period of months they fine-tuned a battle plan, Fall Gelb, which, far more than French bickering and wavering, was to make the real difference. The plan went through four iterations, all of which envisioned a massed armor attack. What varied was the locus of the main thrust, the first three versions fixing it north of the Ardennes as the French had anticipated all along. Indeed, thanks to a remarkable intelligence coup, the French got wind of just these early plans. Hitler, it will be remembered, wanted to invade in November 1939 but agreed to a postponement until the following January, which was still a crazy idea given the winter weather conditions. On the eve of the scheduled assault, a German aircraft carrying an officer in possession of the battle plan veered off course in heavy fog and crash-landed on Belgian territory at Mechelen. Belgian intelligence services captured and interrogated the officer, getting a clear look at where German operational thinking then stood, and that information found its way eventually into French hands. It is not certain that the Mechelen incident caused the Germans, their scheme of attack now revealed, to adjourn their invasion plans yet again, but for whatever reason they did in fact decide in favor of further delay. Hitler now began to reconsider how he wanted the German offensive to play out and in this he was abetted by General Erich von Manstein, a senior officer but not a member of the general staff. It was Manstein (in collaboration with Guderian) who concocted the idea of an invasion through the Ardennes, an idea judged reckless enough by the general staff itself that General Halder did what he could to sideline Manstein. Manstein reached the Führer by back channels, and Hitler, true to his own impulsive nature, liked what the general proposed. In February 1940 the Manstein variant of Fall Gelb was adopted as official policy, and the German general staff, Halder included, then made the scheme their own.[24]

It was a high-risk operation to say the least. The Ardennes were not hospitable to tanks, and in the course of the actual invasion a massive traffic jam developed, exposing the German strike force to potentially devastating aerial bombardment. As for securing bridgeheads on the Meuse, all the daring and initiative of the very best German troops were required to accomplish this. It helped first that the Germans outnumbered the French on the spot by forty-five divisions to eighteen, and that the troops the Germans were facing were not of top quality.[25] Two French armies were stationed on the Ardennes front, General Charles Huntziger's 2nd Army and General André Corap's 9th Army, composed in good measure of reservists and greenhorns. Hitler's decision to attack here was inspired, but not so much so that any of the Führer's generals were ready to predict a certain, let alone crushing, German victory.

No, it required considerable French assistance to make that outcome happen, assistance that came first in the form of a fateful misstep on the part of General Maurice Gamelin, commander of France's armies at the outbreak of the war. Efforts have been made in recent years to refurbish Gamelin's reputation. He was no doubt a top-flight organizer who had conceived an overall defensive scheme that had a good chance of success and who had made sure that the army had the military means—the arms and men—to carry it out.[26] Even so, it is hard to find a good excuse for the decision he took in the spring of 1940 to make adjustments to France's battle plan.

French military strategists never doubted that the main thrust of the German attack would come from the north. The Belgian army might slow down such an assault but could not stop it without French backup, and this the French meant to supply. The initial plan called for sending motorized French units northward no further than the Escaut River, there to staunch a German advance already slowed but not halted by Belgian resistance along the Albert Canal and Dyle River. Once the war got started, however, the Belgians acted to beef up their own defenses with such speed that Gamelin became convinced he would have time to deploy French troops all the way to the Dyle River itself, and in November orders were issued to that effect. So far so good. The Mechelen affair dispelled whatever residual doubts may have lingered about the locus of the German main thrust, emboldening Gamelin to pursue a yet more ambitious scheme. Once the German assault got started, he now envisioned racing an entire army, in the event General Henri Giraud's 7th Army, all the way to Breda in Holland, just north of the Belgian/Dutch border. If the north was to be the scene of the main fighting, why not have some of France's best units near at hand? As Gamelin saw it, the so-called Breda variant also promised political dividends not to be passed up. There was always nagging doubt about how much cooperation to expect from the Belgians in the event of war, but above all from the ultra-neutralist Dutch. Gamelin wagered that the transfer of Giraud's army to the Dutch/Belgian frontier would in a quite literal way induce France's hesitant northern neighbors to get in line under French command. And extending the line that much further northward might be reassuring to France's English ally as well. The Breda variant would guarantee the security of the English Channel, all of it and not just a part, and so insure the home islands against the dangers of cross-Channel invasion.[27]

Why the gambit was such a mistake is not hard to explain, above all with the benefit of hindsight. Giraud's army, initially stationed near Reims, was made up of some of France's "most mobile and modern units." Imagine such a force available for counter-attack against Germany's charge across the Meuse. An over-confident Gamelin, however, deployed the 7th Army well to the north, leaving the front stripped of reserves in what turned out to be the decisive sector. Gamelin's subordinates from his second-in-command, General Alphonse Georges, on down understood the risks and remonstrated against the plan, but Gamelin would not be deterred.[28]

France at the outbreak of the war in 1939 had stood a fair chance of winning. The odds slimmed, however, in the months that followed. Waiting on events had not helped, nor had the distractions of the Norwegian expedition. Yet what made the biggest difference were changes in battle plan undertaken on both sides. Hitler embraced the Fall Gelb, Gamelin the Breda variant. More than anything else, it was senior-level military decision-making, German as well as French, that set France up for defeat.

Yet, even so, this did not mean that the outcome of the Battle of France was decided in advance. It still had to be fought, and in the fighting the French had opportunities to turn the situation around.

CHAPTER 4

LIGHTNING WAR

France's battlefield failings were numerous: sluggish decision-making, deficient improvisational skills, poor communications. These were the result of flawed, indeed blundering, decision-making on the part of the nation's military leadership. It was the army command that lost the Battle of France, not civilian error or a disinclination to fight, let alone faults, real or imagined, in French society as a whole.

The Germans' conduct of the battle must first be given its due. Hitler's armies made bold diversionary moves in the north, and these worked better than the Wehrmacht brass had any reason to expect. Airborne assaults against Dutch and Belgian defenses resulted in rapid victories. The Dutch hadn't wanted to cooperate with anyone, not the French, nor even the Belgians. Hitler sent paratroop units against them, cutting them off before Giraud's 7th Army arrived and then choking them into capitulation, which took just days to accomplish. The fighting began in the early hours of 10 May, and it was over for the Dutch on 15 May. The Belgians held up better but not by much. A daring glider assault captured what were thought to be near-impregnable fortifications on the Albert Canal; the Belgians had to fall back to the Dyle line much sooner than planned for; and then the Belgian king, never keen on the war to begin with, opted for surrender on 28 May without so much as consulting the French who were now supposed to be allies.[1]

The Belgians and Dutch hid out from the reality of the Nazi threat until the very last minute. Yet in the history of "the strange defeat" they have received a free pass, whereas the French were taxed at the time and have been since with failures of all kinds. The capitulations of 15 and 28 May, moreover, are reminders that 1940 was not just a French but also an Allied defeat and that France's responsibility for it needs to be measured accordingly. That said, what mattered most of all was not what happened in the north but what happened in the Ardennes, and here the French had no one to blame but themselves.[2]

The Germans were every bit as daring there, on the Ardennes front, as they had been against the Dutch and Belgians further to the north. It took just a matter of days to move attacking Panzer armies through the forest. The Meuse was then crossed at three spots: by General Hermann Hoth's armored corps at Dinant, General Georg-Hans Reinhardt's at Monthermé, and Guderian's at Sedan. The Monthermé crossing did not go well, hampered by the rugged terrain and the determined resistance of French troops. It looked like the same might happen at Dinant, but the commanding officer on the scene, General Erwin Rommel, took matters in hand. Tanks were called down to the water's edge and from there fired straight across, demolishing French pillboxes on the other side and allowing German engineers, working at a fevered pace, to construct a pontoon bridge.

It was the fighting at Sedan, however, that showed off to best advantage what the German military was capable of. The Luftwaffe threw all it had at the enemy, Stuka dive-bombers subjecting the French defensive line to hours of demoralizing bombardment. Rommel had deployed Panzers against French positions on the opposing shore; Guderian made use of flak units that were instructed to lower their guns, training them, not at the sky, but horizontally at the enemy on the far side of the Meuse. German commandos then traversed the river in rubber dinghies, establishing bridgeheads, which were consolidated by elite units of the Grossdeutschland regiment. And last of all came the tanks.

On the French side, the bombing sowed panic among the inexperienced troops. The shrieking of the Stukas was by all accounts terrifying. Rumors of an impending Panzer assault spread along the front, and in some instances the rumor itself, even in the absence of actual Panzers, sufficed to cause French troops to bolt. News of the disarray reached General Georges's headquarters in the early hours of 14 May, casting a pall on all assembled. "The atmosphere [was] one of a family keeping vigil over a dead member," as one eyewitness recalled. Georges reported to subordinates what had happened, turned pale, and then slumped into an armchair, silenced by a sob.[3] This was warfare of a sort the French had never encountered before, and they were flattened by it.

There is no denying the boldness of the German attack, but note how close run the initial encounters were. Reinhardt's crossing stalled. The attack at Dinant might have ended up the same way had it not been for Rommel's improvisational skills. The fighting at Sedan was a more unmitigated success, but that was thanks not only to Guderian's daring and to the crushing firepower brought to bear on the French but also to the very poor quality of the French troops Guderian confronted—a fortunate coincidence for the German commander.

Demoralizing as the initial breakthrough was, it wasn't fatal in itself. It is what happened next that turned defeat along a narrow stretch of front into an event yet more catastrophic. The French made efforts to contain the German advance, all of which failed (more on that in a moment), leaving Guderian's path to the Channel coast open. He was hell-bent on an all-out dash westward, but General von Kleist, Guderian's commanding officer, ordered him to stop. Kleist worried about a French flanking attack from the south and wanted to allow the infantry time to move up in order to consolidate the gains made by Guderian's armor. Guderian, however, contrived to circumvent the order, hurtling pell-mell toward the Channel instead, an act of insubordination that luckily for him paid off. The rapidity of the advance cut off the British and French armies stationed in Belgium from the bulk of Allied armies further to the south, in effect slicing Allied forces in two.[4] This made possible a crushing victory over France of a kind the Wehrmacht had not anticipated.

For however audacious the German strategy, it is important not to mythologize it. Hitler's military planners hadn't imagined flooring the French with a single hammer blow. They hoped for a victory, to be sure, but one that would send the French reeling and afford German armies a foothold on the Channel coast, the better to turn on

Britain. In this sense, the Germans too were thinking in terms of a drawn-out conflict, of a long war. It was not until Operation Barbarossa in June 1941 that the kind of combined operations employed in the Ardennes were promoted from a battle plan into an overall strategy designed to obliterate the Soviet enemy at a stroke. In France, the Wehrmacht scored just such a knockout victory, but it was unexpected, as much the result of Guderian's freelancing as of the brilliance and clairvoyance of German strategy.

Germany's achievement may not have been quite the stuff of legend, but it was remarkable all the same. Just as remarkable, though, was French bungling. In an era of aerial surveillance, it was impossible to transport massive Panzer armies through the Ardennes without the enemy noticing. French intelligence did indeed take photographs of the tank traffic jam that ensued, sharing them with 9th Army headquarters, but French commanders, convinced that the main attack was coming from elsewhere, refused to believe the evidence.[5]

More serious than this, though, in fact most serious of all, was the French failure to mount an effective counter-attack once the Germans had managed to get to the other side of the Meuse. The absence of adequate reserves explains the failure in part, but just in part. Of equal importance was the French military's general slowness to react. Guderian's attack at Sedan hit French lines at the juncture where Corap's 9th Army and Huntziger's 2nd Army met. Both generals mustered efforts to push the Germans back, Corap taking the first stab. He charged General Pierre Lafontaine, a capable tank commander, with the task, but Lafontaine lost precious time waiting on orders and putting an attack column together. He was supposed to go on the offensive the evening of 13 May but ended up postponing until the next morning, and when he did at last move, he was thinking more of containment than of storming at the enemy. The French command then called in airpower to hammer at the Germans, but the decision was taken late, allowing Guderian time to get flak guns into place. The flak fire blunted the aerial assault, in the process downing 41 of the 71 RAF bombers that had been dispatched to the battle zone.[6]

Slowness of reflexes, though, does not tell the whole story. France's 2nd Army remained intact. Huntziger had the firepower to do something and in the end got around to taking action, but the gesture was half-hearted at best, with French commanders on the scene revealing themselves all too willing to relapse into the defensive mode. Guderian's Panzer corps, having crashed across the Meuse and parried Lafontaine's counterstroke, wheeled to speed westward. Its southern flank now lay exposed, though just for a moment, to Huntziger's 2nd Army. Units of the 2nd Army, including an armored division, were marshaled for an all-out effort, preparing an attack just where Guderian was most vulnerable. The French commander in charge, General Jean Flavigny, had difficulty, however, assembling the strike force because of poor communications with subordinates and fueling problems with the tanks. He was ready at last to move on 15 May, but initial skirmishes with anti-tank units of the Grossdeutschland regiment upset the timing of Flavigny's assault. He regrouped but now hesitated to commit to a full-scale attack. The tank units that did go into action fought well but lacked the concentrated punch to break through. At the end of a day of see-saw fighting, a cautious Flavigny decided to settle into defensive positions. This suited Huntziger, who misjudged German intentions, believing that the enemy wanted to turn the Maginot Line rather than head westward toward the sea. And it was a yet greater relief to the Germans, who appreciated more than French commanders how precarious the German position had been. General Hoth, writing after the war, acknowledged that the French had had a fair chance of winning that day. "Flavigny's counterattack," he noted, "conducted in a resolute manner, would have transformed defeat into victory." But Flavigny was not resolute, reverting to the defensive when it was an offensive posture that was called for. Guderian, now unhindered, sped away en route to the Channel.[7]

This was the moment that the Battle of France was lost.[8] There were further attempts to deflect the German advance, to be sure. At Montcornet (about 40 miles west of Sedan), de Gaulle struck at the still-exposed left flank of Guderian's tank columns as they raced by. This was just the sort of maneuver Kleist had worried about, and de Gaulle's attack was indeed a success, but it lacked sufficient firepower to knock the enemy off course.

Then, as the Germans neared the coast, one last desperate push was made, a combined Franco-British affair. The idea was for French and British units stationed in Belgium to launch a joint operation south-west into France, hitting the Germans this time on their right flank along the Arras–Cambrai line. It was the British military, fearing the imminent entrapment of the British Expeditionary Force, that promoted the plan, the Chief of Staff, General Edmund Ironside, heading to the continent in person to line up French support. He met on 20 May with General Gaston Billotte, commander of France's 1st Army group, but the man Ironside encountered—a worn-out sexagenarian too broken in spirit to take any initiative—left Ironside in a fury. His diary recounts what happened next: "I lost my temper and shook Billotte by the button of his tunic. The man is completely beaten." Billotte's second-in-command, General Georges-Marie-Jean Blanchard, was more self-possessed and promised to muster a smallish force (generaled, as it happened, by the intrepid Jules Prioux) to back the British up.[9] The assault came off on 21 May and to devastating effect. Rommel's Panzer corps lost more tanks that day than in any preceding encounter. The BEF showed its mettle, but this effort, like de Gaulle's, amounted to too little, too late.[10]

What is most striking in this account of France's defeat is the rigidity of thinking in the French military's highest ranks. Generals such as Gamelin, Corap, and Huntziger knew what was supposed to happen, and when the battle did not unfold according to plan they were slow to adjust. Even when adjustments were made there was a tendency to relapse into default mode, which was the defensive. This set of attitudes—the inflexibility of mind, the all too deliberate decision-making, the preference for circling the wagons *faute de mieux*—bled down the chain of command. Not every senior officer was affected, not de Gaulle of course nor Jules Prioux, but enough of them were to make a difference.

It did not help speed up decision-making that communications were so complicated and hierarchical.[11] Gamelin set up his headquarters at Vincennes to the east of Paris. The next in the chain of command was General Georges based further toward the front at La-Ferté-sous-Jouarre on the Marne. Georges commanded Billotte, who in turn commanded Blanchard, Corap, Giraud, and Huntziger. Front-line officers such as Flavigny, Lafontaine, and de Gaulle were yet one rung or more further down the ladder. There were face-to-face exchanges, but orders were on the whole conveyed by field telephone. As the French waited for information to filter its way up and down the hierarchy, German generals took the initiative. At Dinant, as we have seen, Rommel took personal command of the situation, leading from the front, rather than from field headquarters in the rear,[12] while Guderian went one step further, making it up as he went along to the point of insubordination.

Then there were France's tactical shortcomings. It was not as though the French military had failed to understand the importance of tanks and aircraft to modern warfare; it just didn't know how to use them as effectively as Hitler's generals. German tanks massed and swarmed pell-mell, preserving a semblance of coordinated action thanks to radio contact. Not so French tanks, which were deployed in line and required visual communication to remain in touch. In the air, the Germans used bombing in combination with Panzer attack to devastating effect. The French tried to answer back. Strikes against German forces along the Meuse, however, did not succeed—German anti-aircraft fire was just too effective—and after that the Luftwaffe gained air superiority. Airpower had been a weak suit, and now it grew weaker still. It's not that the French hadn't manufactured enough planes, but many of them were not yet battle ready and spent the war on the ground waiting to be tested. A portion of France's air fleet, moreover, was never committed to the fight but kept in reserve to protect North Africa.[13] Britain might have been more helpful in the air war, but it was focused on long-range bombing of the Ruhr and, for the rest, on conserving its fighter fleet to protect Britain itself. In all fairness, the RAF fought hard in the Battle of France, losing an estimated nine hundred planes. Had Britain committed yet more of its fighters, the outcome in all likelihood would have been the same, and the additional squadrons sacrificed on the continent would not then have been available for the forthcoming Battle of Britain, with perhaps disastrous consequences. The French, or the French and British together, had the mechanized firepower they needed. The problem was that they just did not know what to do with it.

France's defeat in 1940 was a military phenomenon, not the inevitable expression of some generalized national malaise or moral deficiency. And it was the army brass, far more than the common fighting man, who deserve the lion's share of the blame. To be sure, front-line units at

Sedan broke and ran. On the other hand, as has been pointed out, the Maginot Line held. It was an extraordinary feat that the BEF remnant, along with tens of thousands of French soldiers, contrived to escape to England via Dunkirk, even while penned in by an enemy boasting air supremacy. Part of the explanation lies in the Führer's decision not to press the attack, whether because he felt the Luftwaffe by itself was up to handling the situation or because he worried about a counter-attack from Allied armies to the south. But part of the answer also lies in the fierce rearguard resistance put up by French armies, trapped within the Dunkirk pocket, which held the line against the Germans at Lille while the BEF prepared its getaway.[14]

Even after defeat along the Meuse and in Belgium, the French soldiered on. Reynaud relieved Gamelin of command on 19 May, replacing him with the far more energetic, though even older, Maxime Weygand. With France's first line of defense near collapse, the new generalissimo set about improvising a second one along the Somme and Aisne rivers. The French had begun to assimilate the lessons of Germany's first attack and prepared a defense in depth; the French aircraft industry had been working full-out in the meantime, with the result that the Luftwaffe's air advantage was diminished. The German attack came in June, and it was stopped dead in its tracks for a couple of days. The French, however, were now outnumbered two to one, and the army command had to order a retreat from the Somme on 9 June and from the Aisne the following day.[15] Weygand's armies reeled backward to the Loire, and, complicating an already deteriorated situation yet further, the Italians then decided to get into the fray. Mussolini, sensing France's impending defeat and hankering for a portion of the spoils, launched an attack on 10 June. Admittedly, the Italian army was not comparable to the Wehrmacht, but Mussolini's attack was a low blow against a France already doubled over, and the Italian dictator might well hope under the circumstances to gain an advantage. But French defenders were well prepared and gave a good account of themselves, fighting the Italian army to a standstill.[16]

The Battle of France was now just about over. Reynaud wanted to fight on, but he met with opposition from elements in his cabinet and, buckling to it, resigned on 16 June, turning the reins of power over to Marshal Pétain. Pétain aired a radio speech on 17 June, which informed the public of plans to seek armistice terms from the Germans and called on French armies in the field to stop fighting. The armistice itself was signed on 22 June.

France's armies had not rolled over in the face of the German onslaught. Indeed, in the space of just six weeks, France had lost 90,000 soldiers killed, this in a nation of just over 40 million souls, a casualty rate that is a moving indicator of the common soldier's will to fight.[17]

Still, it was a defeat and a catastrophic one at that. Catastrophic but not, as Marc Bloch called it, "strange," for there was nothing singular in what happened to France. It was not the sole country to experience defeat in the first years of the war. The Dutch and Belgian debacles in 1940 were yet more ignominious than the French. Britain, though driven from the continent, kept itself together, but then went on to a string of setbacks from Singapore (against the Japanese) to North Africa. The US chalked up its own defeats at the hands of the Japanese, starting with Pearl Harbor and then moving on to the Philippines. As for the Soviet Union, it was almost shattered by Operation Barbarossa. It's not a happy story: Britain and the US underestimated Japanese military capabilities, and everyone underestimated Hitler's Germany. Against such a somber backdrop, do France's battlefield failings stand out in much greater relief than those of anyone else?

France was beaten by the Germans but put up a good fight. Its fate was not so different from that of others who squared off against Axis armies in the war's first years; and what sealed France's defeat was not a failure of national nerve or character as much as poor operational and tactical decision-making on the part of the nation's military elite.

It may be, though, that such a finding still doesn't let France off the hook altogether, for isn't a national army always a reflection of the nation it fights for? And from this premise, doesn't it follow, in light of France's military collapse in 1940, that there must have been something wrong with French society as a whole? The point has some merit. How policy-makers sized up the nation and its capabilities had a real effect on military planning. The French did not want to fight another war like 1914–18, and so a defensive strategy was favored. This was meant to deter the nation's enemies and, in case deterrence failed, to minimize France's casualties. The French army, moreover, was by long-standing tradition a citizen army, made up in large part of conscripts and reservists who did not always have the best training. That was the human material the army brass had to deal with, and they planned accordingly, not demanding too much of soldiers who had limited experience. De Gaulle cast the situation in the harshest light: a stagnant Third Republic threw its weight behind a military doctrine that was "static" in conception. A variant on this theme has been proposed by Tony Judt. He has made the argument that a nation gets the generals it deserves, and by that measure, France's defeat in 1940 was a judgment on France itself.[18]

I don't find these criticisms compelling. On the matter of military doctrine, as we have seen, it was not as though

France's allies and partners had any better strategy to recommend than that of France itself. Indeed, the Dutch, Belgians, and Americans still nurtured hopes in 1939 that they might escape a reckoning with the Nazi war machine altogether. As for the British, more clued in to the necessity of taking the Germans on, they were fully on board with French plans and, even in the wake of France's defeat, continued looking for ways to avoid a head-on clash with Hitler's armies. And was French doctrine so flawed in the first place? I have argued that France's long-war strategy—hold the line, build up resources, then go on the attack—was just the strategy that won the war for the Allies in the end. The problem was that France's line of defense, unlike the Channel, the Atlantic, or the Russian steppes, did not hold. Now, when it comes to generalship, armies—much as other large-scale institutions, universities included—have internal cultures, not independent of the wider national setting but connected to it in complicated, even oppositional ways. A cadre of first-rate generals is not of necessity proof positive of the high moral caliber or even general efficiency of the surrounding society. Take Nazi Germany itself as an example. Hitler's armies were well led and fought with exceptional ferocity to the very end. Is that evidence of National Socialism's superiority as a social system?

A military defeat, however, is never just military but always has a political dimension, and it's when politics are added into the equation that the real strangeness of the French case stands out. France was not the only nation to confront military catastrophe in the first years of the war. Holland capitulated, but its queen, Wilhelmina, then went into exile in England. The Belgians dealt with the situation a little differently, the Belgian government heading across the Channel while King Leopold remained on national soil. Britain itself gave some thought to seeking an armistice. The issue was debated in a series of cabinet meetings in late May. Lord Halifax, still foreign secretary, pushed for Britain to sound out Hitler on possible terms, while the still new prime minister, Churchill, argued not so much against as for a more temporizing course: soldiering on now to show the Germans what kind of fight the British could put up, in the hope of getting a better deal later when the time came to strike a bargain. Once Churchill settled into office, however, and the nation rallied to him, he charted a more determined, win-the-war course, and there was no further talk of negotiation.[19] As for the Soviet Union, a deal was never a realistic option. The Nazis meant to destroy the communist state, and Stalin had no choice but to hang on, a feat he managed to carry off, pulling himself and the USSR together despite devastating initial setbacks.

What did France do by comparison? The French government in 1940 decided to abandon the fight and sue for an armistice, and once the armistice was in place, to remain in the hexagon and undertake an overhaul of the nation's political institutions. This package of decisions *was* unique to France, and in this sense the defeat does say something and something important, not just about France's military but about the Third Republic itself. The regime had a fatal flaw, but it's not the one often identified. No doubt, French politics were divisive and the members of its political class all too often undistinguished, but what counted most in 1940 was the conduct of the nation's military and administrative elites. They had never much liked the Republic and found in the political crisis consequent on defeat an opportunity to exploit the regime's weaknesses against it, to do it in and replace it with an authoritarian order more to their satisfaction.

PART III

DEATH COMES TO
THE REPUBLIC

CHAPTER 5

ARMISTICE

France's Chamber of Deputies and Senate met in joint session on 10 July. The setting was Vichy, a spa town in the Auvergne. The assembled representatives authorized Marshal Pétain to draft a new constitution and to govern with a free hand in the interim, and they did so by a crushing majority: 569 voices in favor with just 80 opposing and 20 abstentions. This was an awful and spectacular act of political "hara-kiri,"[1] a suicide all the more appalling because it cleared the path for a new, authoritarian order to emerge. How had it come to this?

The political collapse of the Third Republic was a tragedy in two acts. The first opened on 5 June when the Germans launched an assault on the Somme–Aisne line. They met with stiff initial resistance but then broke through, pitching toward Paris. The French government was obliged to abandon the capital on 10 June and beat a retreat to the provinces. It relocated to the Touraine, just south of the Loire, a natural barrier which, it was hoped, might provide beleaguered decision-makers with a moment to recoup. Once there, Premier Reynaud convened a series of cabinet meetings at the château de Cangy, and the prospect of an armistice, already a subject of simmering differences, was confronted head-on. Reynaud was dead set against giving up the fight and cast about for alternatives. Winston Churchill flew to the region for a pair of summit talks—Supreme War Councils as they were called—hoping to stiffen French resolve. All the debate, often tense and tempestuous, did not result in a concerted course of action, nor did it slow the German advance. On 14 June a second government transplantation was improvised, this time to Bordeaux. Being a port city, it was well situated for further relocations. Indeed it was from there that a diehard Charles de Gaulle would fly into London exile on 17 June, and that a boatload of no less resolute parliamentarians would sail on the passenger liner *Massilia* en route to French North Africa on 21 June. Yet prior to all such departures Reynaud himself had thrown in the towel. He had hoped the United States might come to France's rescue, but it would not, a demurral made crystal clear to him by the American ambassador's second-in-command, Freeman Matthews, on the morning of 16 June. Reynaud resigned that very day in favor of Marshal Pétain, who was standard-bearer of the pro-armistice faction.

The second act of the drama was less compressed than the first but not by much, unfolding across a span of three and a half weeks from Pétain's accession to office through the vote of 10 July. Pétain addressed the nation on multiple occasions during this period, and it became clear that he meant not just to bring hostilities to a close, but to take charge. On the matter of the armistice, Hitler gave a lending hand, setting terms that were intended to be hard to swallow but not too hard, leaving intact France's empire and fleet, the building blocks of French hopes for a return to greatness. The armistice was in due course signed on 22 June. Britain too in its way helped out. It was not reassured that the French navy was secured against an eventual German takeover and, to be on the safe side, insisted that the battle fleet anchored in the Algerian harbor of Mers el-Kebir set sail for a British port. The French commander wouldn't budge, and on 3 July the British opened fire, sinking the fleet and killing 1,200 sailors in the process. The war was now not just over for France but its bridges to its erstwhile ally, Great Britain, had been well and truly burned, affording Pétain yet greater room for maneuver.

The armistice provided for the division of France into two major zones: one in the north, extending down the Atlantic coast, was occupied by the Germans; the other, made up of central and southern France, was not. Bordeaux fell within the occupied zone, and so Pétain's government decamped in search of a new seat for itself, moving first to Clermont-Ferrand and then at the very end of June to Vichy. Vichy was a resort town with plenty of hotel space to house ministries and government personnel. It was also situated in the Auvergne, the political home turf of Pierre Laval, a one-time socialist who had drifted far to the right. He was a hardcore appeaser who had never wanted France to go to war in the first place. Laval volunteered his services to Pétain, promising to bring the Republic's representatives to cede the Marshal the freedom to act that he craved. What is most disturbing is the staggering success Laval had in this enterprise, resulting in the lopsided vote that placed the nation's fate in Marshal Pétain's hands. Pétain used his new-found powers to create a collaborationist dictatorship: Vichy.

By this account, Vichy's emergence was built on a double capitulation: Reynaud's on 16 June and the National Assembly's on 10 July. It may have been the military that was responsible for France's defeat, but it was the Republic's political class, irresolute and beaten, that did in the Third Republic.[2] I don't quite see it this way.

The Republic did not just self-destruct but was cornered into self-destruction. There was an Iago in this tragedy, indeed, many of them, officers and civil servants who felt little if any loyalty to the regime they served, appeasers and right-wingers who, though never more than a minority, exploited a moment of extreme crisis to get the temporary upper hand. That there were well-placed power-grabbers, gleeful at the chance to finish off the Third Republic, does not absolve the men, from Reynaud on down, who should have known better than to yield, but it does invite a reapportionment of blame. Once the moral balance sheet has been recalculated, it will be possible to take a fresh look at the Republic—at its flaws both inbuilt and born of events and how they contributed to the regime's demise in 1940.

Let's begin by taking a closer look at Reynaud's decision on 16 June to turn over the reins of government to Pétain. The decision, of course, was Reynaud's alone, but he came to it after a series of sometimes unnerving and ever more polarized arguments with cabinet members and military brass first in the Touraine and then at Bordeaux. The pro-armistice faction over time grew in number and did its level best to make Reynaud feel that he had no viable option but to ask for a ceasefire. To start with, it is worth asking who these men were and how they pressed their case.

Reynaud had taken office on 21 March, heading a coalition that extended from the center-left Radical Party through the more moderate Alliance Républicaine (Reynaud's own political formation) to the hard-right Fédération Républicaine. General Gamelin for the time being remained in place as supreme military commander. A first reshuffle on 10 May tilted the cabinet to the right, introducing the Fédération Républicaine stalwart, Louis Marin, and a second more ambiguous figure, Jean Ybarnégaray. Marin was a confirmed anti-German who had never believed in appeasement, but Ybarnégaray was something else altogether. For a period, he had militated alongside Marin in the Fédération Républicaine, but he was a Catholic nationalist at heart who welcomed General Franco's coup against the Spanish Republic in 1936 and wound up bolting from the Fédération Républicaine in favor of Colonel François de La Rocque's Parti Social Français (PSF). Ybarnégaray was a bear of a man with an expansive personality, and he was well liked in the Chamber of Deputies, which may explain why Reynaud appointed him. But the PSF was an authoritarian, far-right party, and it did not augur well for the Republic that a man with such connections had an influential voice in determining its fate.[3]

More fateful by far, however, was the personnel over-haul that unfolded over the three-day period from 17 to

19 May. French lines had been breached on the Meuse, and Reynaud felt an acute need to show a firm hand and boost morale. On 17 May he recalled General Weygand to Paris, the first step en route to promoting him to commander-in-chief, a process consummated two days later when Gamelin got word he was sacked and Weygand was to take his place. In the meantime, on 18 May, Reynaud moved Georges Mandel over from the Ministry of Colonies to the Ministry of the Interior, at the same time bringing Pétain into the cabinet for the first time. It's not hard to figure out what Reynaud thought he was doing. Mandel and Weygand were confident, dynamic men who might be counted on to steady a situation gone awry, and there was a symbolism to the trio of appointments meant to reassure the public. Pétain, of course, was the nation's greatest living war hero, the victor of Verdun, but Mandel and Weygand had also played a part in the Great War, the former as Georges Clemenceau's right-hand man, the latter as Marshal Foch's. Reynaud's message was clear enough: the stalwart men who had brought victory in the Great War were once again at the helm either in person or at one remove.

Reynaud's reshuffle, however, entailed taking a political risk, though not so far as Mandel was concerned. He was a staunch republican cast in the same iron mold as his mentor, Clemenceau. Pétain, renowned for his glacial manner and imperturbability, was harder to figure out. He was a conservative man and a deep-dyed anti-communist, but there was no reason as yet to think he was lacking the will to carry on the war. That would change, of course, as the battlefield reverses piled up. By 26 May, Pétain had begun to doubt the wisdom of fighting to the last man. It would be "criminal" to do so, he expostulated to a confidant on that day, and in almost the same breath he delivered himself of an indictment that betrayed the political direction his thinking had begun to take: "The real guilty party is premier Daladier. He's the one who brought us the Popular Front."[4] In the case of Pétain, a pro-armistice leaning went hand in hand with an ever more encompassing animus against the left. The true political wild card, though, was the septuagenarian Weygand, and there was no doubt about that. He was a known anti-Dreyfusard, not surprising perhaps in a career officer of his generation. In the 1930s, Weygand had sympathized with anti-parliamentary rioters in February 1934 and at decade's end he was connected with military conspirators plotting to rescue a France they felt was too much in thrall to leftist politicians.[5] However effective a military commander Weygand may have been, he was no republican, and as defeat loomed, he grew yet more exalted in his reactionary views. When the Somme–Aisne line broke, he feared that the far left might exploit the situation to seize power in a

Commune-like uprising. It was to forestall just such an eventuality that he opposed the government's departure from Paris in early June, and once the government had removed itself to the Touraine, Weygand continued in the same vein, retailing rumors of a communist coup in the capital that the better-informed and less obsessive Mandel had to dispel.[6] Pétain showed his colors in confidential remarks, but Weygand was not so reticent. At a cabinet meeting on 5 June he let fly, exculpating the army and blaming France's predicament on "twenty years of errors, twenty years of negligence." It was the nation's pacifist schoolteachers, he ranted, and not its generals, who deserved rough handling.[7] Later in the meeting Weygand, now joined by a Marshal Pétain at last ready to show his hand, urged Reynaud to ask for terms from the enemy. Reynaud had wanted to wrap his government in the mantle of Great War heroism, but what he got instead was a pair of military men fixated on scapegoating the left, even as they called for an end to the fighting.

Reynaud's last cabinet reorganization, undertaken that very same day, 5 June, only aggravated the situation.[8] The Dunkirk evacuation had just ended, and the time had come to dig in behind the Somme–Aisne line. Reynaud took the opportunity to clear out a number of defeatist ministers, the notorious Anatole de Monzie among them. At the same stroke, however, he dismissed the minister of foreign affairs, Daladier, who was a personal rival no doubt but also a reliable voice in favor of carrying on the war. Reynaud took over Daladier's position, adding to his own already considerable portfolio of responsibilities. He was prime minister, minister of defense (since 18 May), and now minister of foreign affairs. Reynaud contrived to lighten his burdens by appointing junior ministers to help him out. The post of under-secretary of defense went to Charles de Gaulle, who needs no introduction, and that of under-secretary for foreign affairs to Paul Baudouin, who had been attached to the prime minister's office since March and was a known quantity to Reynaud. Rounding out the list of new cabinet officers were two first-time ministers, Yves Bouthillier at the Ministry of Finance and the press baron Jean Prouvost at the Ministry of Information.

The newcomers were a capable crew, no doubt. Prouvost apart, all were young stars on the rise, reputed for their brilliance and administrative skills. De Gaulle, a graduate of the national military academy at Saint-Cyr, was a proven and innovative battlefield commander. Baudouin and Bouthillier both belonged to the prestigious state administrative corps, the Inspectorat des Finances. None of the four new cabinet members, moreover, was a politician. Not Prouvost the businessman; not de Gaulle the career officer and apostle of army professionalism; not Bouthillier and

Baudouin the experts in public administration. Reynaud in so selecting may have thought he was bringing in a non-partisan cadre of the best and the brightest, but he was mistaken. Three of the new men (de Gaulle was the exception) had come recommended by Reynaud's mistress Hélène de Portes. She, unlike her more steadfast inamorato, had attached herself to the pro-armistice camp, and her three protégés thought much as she did. It's not only that most of the new men favored getting out of the war but that a couple of them—Baudouin and Bouthillier—were not republicans at all. The former was a "fervent Christian" well disposed to the corporatist experiments of the Salazar regime in Portugal. He liked the idea of Weygand as a potential successor to Reynaud and did not hesitate to confide in the generalissimo, lamenting to him in a private conversation in late May that France had lost its way: "The moral force of this country has been reduced to ruins ... What we need is a thorough-going labor of reconstruction."[9] As for Bouthillier, he has been described as "a disciple of Maurras, if not an out-and-out Action française militant." He was an enemy of the Popular Front, an appeaser, and an Anglophobe.[10]

As the military situation deteriorated, Reynaud made repeated efforts to shore up his government, surrounding himself with the most storied figures of the French establishment and with a raft of younger men of exceptional energy and executive capacity. At the same time, he unwittingly reinforced the pro-armistice faction and, even worse, introduced into the councils of power not just *mous* but proto-authoritarians who hated the left and had little more taste for the Republic itself.

This was a recipe for disaster when it came to finding a way forward, and that became evident once French defenses along the Somme–Aisne line began to buckle. At a pair of cabinet meetings on 8 and 9 June, just as the government was preparing to flee the capital, Weygand and Pétain made clear to all present where they stood. The time had come to treat with the enemy. Weygand, as he had before, railed on about "twenty years of abdication," a theme Senator Joseph McCarthy would take up (substituting treason for abdication) in another context fifteen years later, with Pétain chiming in: "This country needs an overhaul top to bottom."[11]

How did Reynaud answer back? First, with the apposite observation that France's enemy in this war was not just any enemy, or as he put it at a cabinet meeting on 12 June: "We're not dealing with Kaiser Wilhelm but with Genghis Khan."[12] Second, he proposed alternatives to surrender: holing up in a so-called Breton redoubt or retreating to North Africa. There was always the possibility, moreover, that the British might yet come to the rescue, dispatching additional fighter squadrons to the continent; or, the most desperate hope of all, that the US would intervene in some unspecified way to save the day. Finally, Reynaud floated what might be called the Dutch option. Holland's armies had capitulated to the conquering Germans, but Queen Wilhelmina and her government had then headed for London, leaving Holland itself in the hands of administrative caretakers. Might not France, Reynaud proposed, do the same?

Most of these options did not get very far. De Gaulle and Churchill liked the Breton gambit, but it was never accorded a serious thinking through, and the rapidity of the German army's advance soon made the whole question moot. Nor was Britain in much of a position to extend aid that might make a difference. As the French government retreated to the Touraine, Churchill flew to France for face-to-face talks. A first meeting took place on 11–12 June, Churchill coming at Weygand's invitation to the château Muguet near Briare; a second took place at Tours on 13 June. Churchill promised just two additional fighter units, pleading by way of excuse that his cabinet, worried about home defense, would authorize nothing more. The French also pressed him on the question of an armistice. France after all was treaty-bound to stand by Great Britain. Would the British let their ally sue for a separate peace? Churchill answered back, urging the French to fight on and suggesting that they sound out Roosevelt.

There were Anglophobes, Bouthillier for example, already in Reynaud's cabinet. Pétain himself had never much cared for the British and made no secret of his views. After the Tours meeting, Anglophobic sentiment gained in currency, and few remained who put much stock in help from that quarter. Churchill made one last desperate effort to turn things around on 16 June. He proposed to de Gaulle, who was on a mission in London at the time, that Britain and France form a union, though how such a gesture, however grand, might work out in practice or improve France's fortunes was not made clear. De Gaulle dutifully phoned in the offer to the French cabinet, which then voted to turn it down by a close margin, 14 to 10. As for the American option, it too came to nothing. Reynaud had acted on Churchill's counsel and petitioned Roosevelt for assistance. Early on 16 June the answer came in. The US conveyed to Reynaud its ongoing moral support but nothing more substantial than that.[13]

There would be no Breton redoubt and no Anglo-American bailout, but France might yet prosecute the war from its empire. Reynaud seized on the idea at Cangy but seems to have been forced to reconsider for two reasons. First of all, the opposition he encountered was ferocious to the point of insubordination. At a first cabinet meeting on 12 June, Pétain raised the stakes in the debate: it would be "criminal," he declared, to wait a moment longer to ask for an armistice, and Baudouin picked up on the theme in a private conversation with Reynaud afterward. "France does not reside in its colonies but in its home soil," Baudouin told the prime minister, adding that it would be a "crime" to leave the nation to the invader's mercy. At a second cabinet meeting the next day, Pétain turned up the pressure yet further. He stood up and read a prepared statement, an unusual procedure, and what he then went on to say just added to the extraordinary nature of the occasion. He himself would never leave metropolitan France. A government that did not stand by its people risked losing legitimacy and, worse, a France abandoned by its natural leaders risked losing its "soul," along with all hope of a future "renaissance." Pétain's words were delivered in measured language even if what he had to say was not so measured. Weygand took the extra step. The general had contempt for politicians, and all the hand-wringing about what course to pursue just exasperated him. He told cabinet members that there was but one choice, armistice, and dodging that basic truth was just proof of a lack of courage. As for leaving France, Weygand went on, he would sooner be clapped in chains, and with that he asked permission to leave, storming out in a fury.[14] The pro-armistice faction made two points plain: that they viewed any other policy as a criminal betrayal and lacking in legitimacy, and that they for their part—by implication in Pétain's case, explicitly so in Weygand's—would not obey any order to move the government and the military to North Africa.

Doubts about the feasibility of the enterprise further eroded Reynaud's resolve. He had been in contact with the commanding officer in North Africa, General Charles Noguès, about the possibility of prosecuting the war from there. Noguès had telegrammed back in discouraging tones: there were not enough men, not enough materiel for the purpose. After the disastrous cabinet meeting of 13 June, Baudouin and Reynaud separately sought out Admiral François Darlan, the navy's most senior officer, to talk through the matter. The question that both put to the admiral was this: was it realistic to think about transporting France's armies in the hexagon to North Africa? Darlan's reply to both was much the same. In the face of German air superiority, such a crossing was unthinkable and North Africa itself undefendable. The exchange prompted Baudouin to a demonization of the anti-armistice camp: they were demagogues, out of touch with the realities of "life": "They have lost contact with French soil." Reynaud's conclusion by contrast was to cast about for a different course of action, and it was at this juncture that he began to explore the Dutch solution.[15]

The scene had by this time shifted to Bordeaux, which was not favorable terrain for Reynaud. The town mayor was Adrien Marquet, a renegade socialist, unrepentant appeaser, and crony of Pierre Laval. Moreover, the numerous refugees and hangers-on who had relocated to Bordeaux seeking safe haven did not scruple to manifest their unhappiness with the politicians they held responsible for their present plight, Reynaud not least among them. This was the setting in which the prime minister fired his last shot, and it proved a blank. First and most important of all, Weygand and Pétain remained unbending. Not long after talking to Darlan, Reynaud tried out the idea of a Dutch alternative on Weygand, who responded with "a formal refusal." He was no less adamant when the cabinet met later that day, and the argument spilled over afterward, growing ever more heated. The generalissimo squared off against Reynaud, insisting once more that he would under no circumstances sign a capitulation. This gave rise to the following exchange, Reynaud speaking first:

> You will do it if I give the order.
> Never ...
> You are here to obey.
> I am here to defend the honor of the army.[16]

Weygand was mutinous. Pétain, by contrast, was more politic, squeezing Reynaud rather than defying him outright. The cabinet met once more early on 16 June, and the Marshal then made his move. He stood up and read a statement threatening to resign, confronting Reynaud with an awkward choice: ask the Germans for terms or fall out with one of France's most prestigious and respected public personalities.

Two further factors weighed on Reynaud's decision. Over the course of the day, the US and Great Britain both had occasion to show how little they could do to help the French out—America by its early-morning formal refusal to intervene, Britain by its futile, last-minute scheme to form a union. France, Reynaud must have concluded, was on its own, and Reynaud himself felt more and more isolated. As the prime minister's room for maneuver narrowed, the cabinet's will to back him slipped in equal measure. He could still count on the support of a half dozen diehards, among them the minister of armaments Raoul Dautry, Mandel and Marin, but the pro-armistice faction had begun to grow. No more than half a dozen at Cangy, they now accounted for a near majority as the fence-sitters and opportunists rallied to their side.[17] The pressure was too much for Reynaud. Unable to stomach the prospect of opening armistice talks himself, he stepped aside in favor of someone who knew no such hesitations—and so Marshal Pétain became prime minister, the Third Republic's last.

It's impossible not to take a dim view of Reynaud's capitulation. He made disastrous personnel choices, in effect creating a pro-armistice bloc—Pétain, Baudouin, Ybarnégaray, Bouthillier, Prouvost—that didn't have to exist. From a political point of view, the most disastrous appointment of all was the rancorous, indeed mutinous Weygand as commander of France's armies in the field. And then Reynaud gave in to the pro-armistice faction when it may be he did not have to. To be sure, Noguès and Darlan had been discouraging about carrying on the fight from North Africa, but why not try?[18] Hitler had had air superiority at the time of Dunkirk, but the BEF had made good its escape all the same and with no advance planning. France might have been able to pull off a similar feat had it acted with a will. Much depended on how the Spanish conducted themselves. Had Franco come to Hitler's aid, he would no doubt have exacted a heavy price—a chunk of France's empire in all likelihood—but think where that would have left Spain and Germany: the former embroiled in a war with Britain and imperial France, not so welcome a prospect whatever the potential gains for a country just emerging from a ruinous civil war; the latter committed to mobilizing an amphibious assault on North Africa, a much more challenging enterprise than an amphibious assault on Great Britain, which in the event it was never able to pull off.

Reynaud let himself be pushed around by overly prudent military men like Noguès and Darlan, and then let himself be bullied in his dealings with Weygand and Pétain. Why not, after all, go the Wilhelmina route and head to North Africa or Great Britain for that matter? The *Massilia* passengers did just that and so too did de Gaulle. It's easy enough, of course, to grasp Reynaud's thinking on this point. The pro-armistice group had made clear, not just that it opposed leaving the hexagon, but that it regarded any such gesture as a betrayal of the national interest and of the French people at a time of extreme suffering. A monarch like Wilhelmina, Bouthillier conceded, might carry the mantle of sovereignty with her, but not a republican head of government who lacked that kind of embodied legitimacy. Pétain had made a similar point to Reynaud at Cangy: a Reynaud government overseas would not be recognized as a government at all by the French people. Such an admonition was bound to give the prime minister pause. Imagine a face-off between Reynaud and Pétain, the former ensconced in North Africa accompanied by a handful of ministers, the latter "with his crown of glory" and backed by Weygand "with his prestige" still on the scene in metropolitan France. It is reasonable to suppose that Reynaud would have come out the loser in any such contest.[19]

Reynaud was not the great man that de Gaulle proved himself to be; he did not brave the odds. It is understandable, however, why Reynaud chose as he did, and he cannot be faulted for having failed to make energetic efforts to find another outcome. One more thing: Reynaud was not choosing in a vacuum. The Germans had him cornered; Great Britain, which accorded justifiable priority to homeland defense, was in no position to help out, nor was a US just starting to emerge from isolationism; and at every turn Reynaud had to push up against an ever bolder pro-armistice faction. An up-close look at that faction and how it conducted itself opens up a second perspective on the crisis of 16 June, focusing not so much on Reynaud's failings as on the character and determination of his enemies.

The pro-armistice faction did not just argue about policy: they were interested in regime change, if not from the very outset, then soon enough. Weygand did not hide the fact that he considered the Third Republic "unworthy."[20] He was more explicit than most, but the themes he sounded were taken up by others. Communism threatened public order; the Popular Front and pacifists had rotted the nation's soul away; France stood in dire need of a spiritual overhaul; and only those in touch with the national soil had the moral weight to bring such a renaissance about. These would in time become Vichy themes, but this comes as little surprise since the men who articulated them, from Pétain on down, were to become Vichy ministers in just a few weeks' time.

These were men of exceptional stature and ability, France's best and brightest, and that's in fact why Reynaud had turned to them in the first place. Yet even if Reynaud can't be taxed with picking incompetents, couldn't he have made wiser choices? Surely there were some in France's military and civil service establishments who were not that unreliable in political terms. No doubt there were, and de Gaulle himself may be cited as a case in point (Reynaud in fact did single out de Gaulle for promotion). Yet de Gaulle was probably more the exception than the rule. In early June, when Reynaud left Paris by car, he was accompanied by de Gaulle who was upset to learn that it was an overreaching Weygand and not Reynaud himself, the head of government, who had invited Churchill to the château Muguet near Briare. Reynaud took the point, making up his mind to sack Weygand and replace him with General Charles Huntziger, a course of action of which de Gaulle approved (and which Reynaud never acted upon).[21] But would Huntziger have been that much sounder a choice? He was a less obstreperous personality than Weygand, to be sure, but he wasn't that distinguished a military commander, as his record at the head of the 2nd Army attests. As for politics, Huntziger was in due course to prove himself a reliable Vichyite. He represented France in armistice negotiations with the Nazis, accepting the German terms that he found "hard but not dishonoring,"[22] and then went on to serve the regime for a period as minister of war. Or consider the examples of Noguès and Darlan, two of the key senior officers who did so much to frame Reynaud's options. In contrast to Weygand, neither was a marked reactionary, but on the other hand neither demonstrated much affinity for democratic institutions over the course of events to come. Not Darlan, of course, who went on to a term of service as Pétain's second-in-command at Vichy. Noguès never reached so high, but he did remain in charge in French North Africa and in that capacity showed no reluctance to order French troops to fire on American soldiers during the Allied invasion of November 1942. When it then came to deciding how to govern a liberated North Africa, moreover, Noguès did not favor de Gaulle, preferring instead the proconsulship of General Henri Giraud, himself a semi-repentant Pétainist. No, the moment Reynaud began looking to appoint non-partisan experts, he was fishing in troubled waters: France's military and civil service elites were that much riven with second thoughts, or worse, about the value and efficiency of democratic institutions.

No less disturbing, Reynaud's so-called experts did not hesitate to play hardball in pursuit of their goals. Bouthillier and Baudouin of course kept low profiles, not making too much noise in cabinet meetings but letting on how they felt when tête-à-tête. Pétain too was no shouter, but his

Olympian manner did not stop him from throwing a thunderbolt or two, rising in cabinet debate to read statements threatening resignation or branding policies favored by Reynaud as criminal. The point man when it came to intimidation was Weygand, who battered the prime minister with fits of temper and fiery defiance, so that Reynaud in the end bent before the onslaught.

From this angle, the 16 June crisis and Pétain's accession to power appear not so much the result of Reynaud's weaknesses (though more might have been hoped for from a man so able) as the result of what amounted to, in one historian's words, "a palace coup."[23] Robert Paxton noted some years ago how well stocked the Vichy regime was with experts, civil servants, and military brass, concluding "to judge Vichy is to judge the French elite."[24] Yet even before Vichy itself was in place, the French elite had begun to turn, and what better evidence to make the point than the conduct of its most haloed, most brilliant representatives in the run-up to 16 June?

Yet doesn't just such a finding nail down once and for all the case against the Third Republic? That is, it was a flawed regime which in the end met with the fate it deserved. No doubt the Republic was flawed but it is critical to keep in mind just what the nature of that flaw was. From its inception in the 1870s to its very end, the regime had had difficulties with the military. France's chief executive in 1877, Marshal Patrice de MacMahon, was no republican but found himself, whether he liked the regime or not, the Republic's president. Confronted with a parliamentary majority he didn't care for, he dismissed parliament on 16 May of that year, the so-called *seize mai* coup. There were fears that MacMahon might go a step further and, military man that he was, engineer an army takeover. The Marshal backed down in the face of determined public opposition, and the crisis was resolved, but uncertainties about the military's loyalty persisted, and for good reason as the behavior of so many senior officers at the time of the Dreyfus Affair bore witness. Yet again, in the 1930s, there were rumblings of military plots against the Republic. One of the reasons why Gamelin was named to the command of France's armies was that he enjoyed a reputation as a soldier whose republican loyalties might be counted on. The army had its own, non-democratic ethos; and it was a refuge for royalists and Catholics who wanted to serve France but had a hard time making peace with a secular Republic.

Nor should it be thought that the French military's political unreliability came to an end with the Third Republic. The Fourth foundered in 1958 under pressure from an army unhappy with the regime's conduct of the Algerian War; and the Fifth in its turn had to face down an attempted putsch in 1961 although it pulled through, unlike its predecessor, thanks to General de Gaulle's sang-froid and political skills. It took a general in the end to teach the nation's generals how to live with a Republic.

It's not so much that the Third Republic was a rotten regime, but that post-revolutionary France was saddled with a military establishment that had not made its peace with democratic institutions and would not do so until the 1960s. If there was a flaw in the regime, it lay not in republican political culture but in a military caste as yet inadequately republicanized.

CHAPTER 6

THE ROAD TO VICHY

The comparison between the *seize mai* crisis of 1877 and the 16 June crisis of 1940 is suggestive, but there was a crucial and telling difference between the outcomes of the two events. The *seize mai* crisis ended in Marshal MacMahon's backing down, a hinge moment in the consolidation of the Third Republic. The 16 June crisis had just the opposite denouement—Marshal Pétain came out on top whereas the Republic went under—and this for one simple reason: in 1877 republicans stood by what they believed in; in 1940 they cut and ran. So maybe Reynaud's capitulation does not provide incontrovertible proof of the regime's bankruptcy, but the National Assembly's suicidal vote on 10 July does.

It's hard not to be swept along by this way of looking at things, but several additional observations need to be made before a final judgment can be rendered. The first has to do with the circumstances under which the decision on 10 July was taken. The 1940 defeat was not just a military collapse but a debacle for France's civilian population as well, who fled by the millions before the Wehrmacht's advance, creating chaos and moral dislocation from which the enemies of the Republic contrived to profit. Then there is the conduct of the Republic's enemies themselves, first Pétain and then Laval—the former from the moment he became prime minister herding France toward an authoritarian solution, the latter by maneuver and threat working in tandem to consummate the process. Last of all, there is the question of what happened to France's political class in the wake of its fateful decision. Second thoughts set in before long, a buyer's remorse that hit sooner and ran deeper than is usually recognized.

A discussion of the exodus is the place to begin. Two million Belgians fled before the onslaught of Hitler's armies, and their numbers were soon swelled by millions more French. Belgium and northern France had had first-hand encounters with the harshness of a German occupation during the Great War, and local residents did not want to relive the experience. Some provision for evacuation had been made, but the planning was modest in scale.

No one anticipated a mass exit of such proportions, and preparing for a worst-case scenario might have been unnerving to civilians anyhow. The worst case happened, nonetheless, and the situation got worse still once the exodus was in full spate. A handful of prefects, the future Resistance hero Jean Moulin among them, and many mayors remained at their posts to face down the approaching enemy, but other officials did not. They may have felt under obligation, as the state's representatives, to avoid capture; they may have been caught up themselves in the climate of panic. Either way, the end result was the same: a breakdown of public services and a widening sense that the authorities had abdicated their responsibilities. The sight of so many soldiers, themselves in flight, added to the general demoralization, and the German military made its own contribution by strafing and bombing refugee columns.[1]

This was a catastrophe by any measure. The exodus and how it was handled—or not—may offer yet one further proof of the Republic's unworthiness.[2] Yet, in all fairness, it's not clear that France's level of unpreparedness, high as it was, was that much higher than anyone else's. What is certain is that the disaster ate away at the public's allegiance to the regime. The deputies and senators who regrouped in Bordeaux were cognizant of the growing disenchantment, "made clear to us," as one of them put it, "on all the streets and the public spaces of the city,"[3] and they would get that feeling again, though this time with yet greater intensity, once they relocated to Laval's home base in the Auvergne.

One figure, however, positioned himself to turn to advantage the regime's discomfiture, and that was Pétain. The Marshal, once head of government, took swift action. He delivered a radio address on 17 June, letting listeners know that he intended to ask Germany for armistice terms. He framed the announcement, however, in a way that drew the nation's legitimating gaze on himself. France was hurting, he explained, and to "attenuate its pain," he was prepared to make to it "the gift of his person." He felt "compassion" and "solicitude" for the "unhappy refugees" who crowded France's roads, and that is why, with a "heavy heart," he was suing for peace. This speech told of the Marshal's sacrifice and deep feeling; three days later, on 20 June, he went on the airwaves again, though this time adopting the tone of a sympathetic but reproving parent. France had won a great victory in 1918 but then frittered it away. Citizens had got into the habit of taking rather than giving; they indulged themselves and did not sacrifice. The result was France's present calamity, and if the nation aspired to greatness again, it would have to learn from its mistakes. This speech lacked the harshness of General Weygand's vituperations about twenty years of demagogy, but it was very much in the same spirit.

Pétain instrumentalized the exodus and the defeat to build himself up as a providential man, a savior and father to whom a people in distress might turn. There was a creeping authoritarianism in such posturing, and the Marshal was abetted in this by the members of his new cabinet. Bouthillier and Prouvost were kept on, and Baudouin got promoted to minister of foreign affairs. A new man, Raphaël Alibert, was brought in as under-secretary of state, and he was every bit as anti-republican as the rest. A jurist who had taught at Sciences Po in the 1930s, Alibert was known to refer to the Republic from the teaching podium as *la gueuse*, the whore. Such men, conferring among themselves and with the Marshal, sketched out the future they imagined for France. Case in point: a note drafted by Weygand, read to and okayed by Pétain, and then communicated on 28 June to a no less approving Baudouin. It was time to finish with the old order of things, the document explained, with its "shopworn personnel," its "Masonic compromises," and its "class struggle." A feeble birth rate had left France prey to foreign interlopers who, exploiting all too lax natural-ization laws, had come to make themselves at home, buying up the nation's wealth along the way. A "wave of materialism" had eroded family values and the morals of youth. The nation needed new leaders and new principles to live by. It was high time to find a replacement for the Republic's outdated motto, "Liberty, Equality, Fraternity," and Weygand had just such a device in mind: "God, Country, Family, Labor." Rebirth, purity, authority, such were the watchwords of the Pétain cabinet, a government that had already left the Republic behind even before it left Bordeaux en route to Vichy.[4]

The new Pétain administration had little sympathy for the republican institutions it had been put in charge of, for parliament, or for the word-spinning politicians who made parliament their home. What was to be done with the lot of them?

Pétain himself had part of the answer: make sure that its ranking representatives did not set up shop in North Africa where they might constitute a competing node of legitimacy. Here's the point at which to take a closer look at the fate of the *Massilia* expedition. On 18 June, Pétain assented to the plan of a number of parliamentarians, including the president of the Republic, Albert Lebrun, to sail for Casablanca. While the Marshal meant to remain on French soil, he did not object to others leaving if they so desired. Such was his initial position. In a matter of days, however, Pétain reversed course, influenced by Alibert who had been hostile to the *Massilia* venture from the outset. Efforts were made to persuade Lebrun to remain: there was no rush to depart, he was told, as German armies were still some distance from Bordeaux; why not wait to find out what Hitler's armistice terms were? And on it went. In case Lebrun remained unconvinced, however, Pétain was prepared to resort to tougher measures. Baudouin, for one, fretted about Lebrun's imminent departure, and he pressed the Marshal on what he planned to do to stop it. "It's very simple," Pétain reassured his minister, "I'll have him arrested,"[5] though in the event this did not prove necessary. Then on the very eve of the *Massilia*'s departure, Pétain rescinded the order to let it go. It sailed away all the same, although it's unclear whether those on board were aware of how the situation had changed. In a matter of days, Pétain's minister of information, Prouvost, was branding the *Massilia*'s passengers as national outcasts, and they would in fact be treated as such.[6] On arrival in Morocco, they were sequestered in a hotel. Mandel, who was among their number, was placed under house arrest, and several others who happened to be army officers as well as deputies—Jean Zay and Pierre Mendès France for instance—were charged with desertion in the face of the enemy.

Pétain used a firm hand to squash the *Massilia* expedition, a foretaste of more authoritarian measures to come, but he did not pull off the maneuver without critical assistance. He got help from three quarters, from Laval first of all. The Bordeaux town hall with Mayor Adrien Marquet's blessing became a gathering place for pro-armistice parliamentarians, Laval in the lead. On 21 June the cabal sent a delegation to buttonhole Lebrun, determined to get him to stay. Laval, who did most of the talking, did not mince words, speaking in a voice that was "curt, authoritarian." He had a string of arguments to make. Weygand and Pétain were in the right, and as military men they understood France's plight better than the likes of a Reynaud or Churchill. Therefore, it was inconceivable that Lebrun, in furtherance of a bankrupt policy, should leave France. As Laval put it "with a sudden vehemence": "I do not recognize your right to leave, whatever the pretext or excuse." Laval pivoted then from indignation to menace to make his final, clinching point. There was, he went on, a word to describe Lebrun's proposed line of conduct: "defection . . . perhaps a word graver still, that of treason."[7]

The upshot of the exchange was twofold. Lebrun caved in, and his about-face weighed on others. Edouard Herriot, the president of the Chamber of Deputies, followed the president of the Republic's example: his luggage went out on the *Massilia*, but he did not. Second of all, Laval was well rewarded for his services. He coveted a position in Pétain's cabinet and on 23 June he got one. He did not become minister of foreign affairs as he wanted—this was more than Pétain, who had no stomach for intriguing politicians, could tolerate—but minister of state, as did Marquet too for that matter. Lebrun had at first refused to sign Laval's appointment but did so in the end on the Marshal's firm insistence.[8]

Helpful as Laval was, it was Noguès who played the more decisive role in scotching the North African gambit. De Gaulle telegrammed the general twice, on 19 and 24 June, appealing to him to rally to the Gaullist cause, and on both occasions Noguès turned a deaf ear.[9] He was not deaf, however, to commands to sequester, arrest, and deport back to France *Massilia* passengers for eventual trial. It was he more than anyone else, moreover, who put a damper on any consideration of creating a North African redoubt. He had discouraged Reynaud on this score and continued in the same vein once Pétain acceded to office. The Marshal, as we have seen, did not want anyone heading out to North Africa, but he had a nagging worry. What if Hitler's terms were unacceptable, unacceptable in this context translating as a threat to the integrity of France's fleet or empire? In that case, maybe some kind of North African operation might be called for after all. Weygand sounded Noguès out about the matter and got an unambiguous reply, which he reported on to a cabinet meeting on 22 June. Senior government officials who relocated to Algiers risked assassination. Offensive operations against Italy in Libya might be possible but not until September. And it would be necessary in the meantime to occupy Spanish Morocco to forestall a German landing there, bringing Spain into the conflict as a result. A liaison officer was dispatched to Algeria to confirm Noguès's assessment. The officer returned the very next day, 23 June, and spelled out the situation in no uncertain terms. Bouthillier came away persuaded that any move in North Africa was not just "chimerical" but "dangerous."[10]

Had Hitler pressed France's plenipotentiaries too hard during the armistice negotiations, the Pétain government might have found itself in an impossible position, torn between accepting the unacceptable or pursuing a North African strategy it had no desire to pursue. But the Führer extended a helping hand, just as Laval and Noguès had done before him. Hitler wanted nothing more than a peaceful southern flank, the better to focus his attentions on finishing off Great Britain, and so the terms he tendered were not intolerable so far as the French fleet and empire were concerned. Indeed, Hitler prevailed on his own military, which had initially envisioned a harsher deal, to take a step back.[11]

This is not to say that the agreement was generous. Quite the contrary: three-fifths of France's continental territory was subjected to an occupation whose costs the

French themselves were obliged to bear; the Germans also occupied (and then later annexed outright) Alsace and the Moselle; captured French soldiers—and there were well over a million and a half of them—were required to remain in POW camps until Germany's war with Britain had ended; and not least of all, the French had to surrender asylum-seekers and German refugees to the Nazis, an ignominious violation of the laws of hospitality. This was a punitive bargain, no doubt, but Hitler compromised on just the points where compromise was called for, and Pétain, who had staked so much on bringing the fighting to an end, swallowed the rest. So an armistice accord was signed on 22 June. A ceasefire went into effect three days later, and the Marshal's government relocated itself to Vichy in the unoccupied zone.

Pétain might well congratulate himself on how much had been accomplished in such a short space of time. He headed a cabinet of like-minded men, most of them hand-picked, with the exceptions of Laval and Marquet. North Africa was quiet and the fleet and empire were still in French hands. Most important of all, France's war was over, the sine qua non of the Marshal's larger objective, a national rebirth under the sign of labor, family, and father-land. This might have been enough for the Marshal. He was already well on the way to establishing the regime of paternal authority he felt was required, but then on 2 July,

Laval dangled the promise of yet greater authority. He would get the National Assembly—the term for the Chamber of Deputies and Senate when they met together—to suspend the constitution, in effect making Pétain not just head of government but the sole and unbounded master of France's destiny (not counting Hitler, far from a minor caveat). Baudouin did not think the idea feasible, but Laval had a ready answer to such hesitations: "You don't have experience. With fear, it is possible to get men to do anything, for they are cowards."[12]

Laval got the go-ahead to win over the National Assembly, and this he did with a degree of success that cannot but be unsettling to friends of democratic institutions. How did he pull it off?

To some extent, Laval was pushing against an open door. The defeat and the exodus, as has been intimated, shook the public's confidence in parliamentary government, a loss of faith that in turn eroded the democratic resolve of the nation's representatives. Many of them, of course, did not need much persuading. Not elements on the right such as the Fédération Républicaine mainstay Pierre-Etienne Flandin who had been accumulating doubts about democracy for some time. Nor a solid phalanx of *mous*, about a hundred in all (not counting pro-peace socialists), who were lined up behind Laval, ready for any maneuver.[13] Circumstances too came to Laval's aid. Britain's decision to sink the French fleet at Mers el-Kebir on 3 July stiffened the Pétain administration's determination to leave the bad old days of the Republic behind, and some deputies and senators were swept along by the anti-British current.

It also needs stressing that the parliamentary voices most likely to take a stand against Laval did not make themselves heard. This is explained in part by absence. One representative in four was unable to take part in the Vichy deliberations. Well over a hundred had been called to the colors and for that reason couldn't attend. Remember also that Communist deputies who had not renounced the party's anti-war line were placed under arrest in 1939 and still remained in detention. And then there were the twenty-six deputies and one senator who had sailed out on the *Massilia* and now found themselves moldering far away in French North Africa. The group included some strong personalities, convinced republicans like Daladier and Mandel and future *résistants* like Mendès France and André Le Troquer. The National Assembly might not have rolled over with such ease had these men been on hand.

Still, it is not as though the Assembly was stripped of all its committed democrats. Reynaud remained on the scene, and so too did Léon Blum, yet they did not speak up. Reynaud's is a special case. He had been in a car accident on 28 June that killed his mistress and left him with a bandaged head. There was a first, preliminary vote on 9 July, the two houses of parliament meeting separately, to sanction a revision of France's constitutional laws. Reynaud attended the Chamber of Deputies meeting and cast a ballot in favor, but he did not take part in the decisive vote the next day when both houses, meeting in joint session, confirmed the need for a change in the constitution and at the same time invested Pétain with full powers. Blum's silence is more troubling. The man did not lack fortitude. Vichy would blame him (among others) for France's misfortunes and place him on trial in 1942 at Riom. The charges were trumped up and the setting—a pro-Vichy courtroom—intimidating, but Blum rose in his own defense and with consummate oratorical skill turned the tables on his accusers. This is not what happened in July 1940, however. Blum voted against constitutional revision on 9 July and against constitutional revision and *pleins pouvoirs* the next day, but he made no eloquent plea justifying his course of action. Blum's Socialist Party was divided with a significant faction favoring a pro-Pétain line, and it may be that Blum did not want to bring the fracture to breaking point. Or it may be that, courageous as he was, Blum felt a moment's fear. He was a socialist and a Jew, the one-time standard-bearer of the Popular Front now so much reviled by the government in power.

The town of Vichy itself was infested with right-wing thugs, and Blum had had a run-in before with such types. Action française toughs had pulled him from a car during the electoral campaign of 1936 and almost beaten him to death. It's worth adding that units of the German army were stationed not 40 miles to the north at Moulins; and Blum did not have much reason to feel reassured knowing that a French division, under Weygand's command, was bivouacked about the same distance to the south at Clermont-Ferrand. Blum himself later spoke of the climate of "fear" that prevailed at Vichy in 1940 and of its decomposing effects.[14]

There is no doubt that Laval, true to his word, played the fear card for all it was worth. Speaking in closed session to the nation's representatives on the morning of 10 July, he stigmatized France's entry into the war as "the greatest crime." He accused Mandel of conspiring with the British "to foment insurrection" and leveled a personal attack on Blum for lack of patriotism. Nor was Laval's bullying just ad hominem. A few days preceding he had addressed a group of eighty deputies, advising them to accept what he proposed or else swallow a constitution imposed by the Germans. He adopted a similar tack dealing with a delegation of veterans hoping to find a way forward more in accord with republican principles. There was no room for compromise, Laval told them: "I will resign, and in that case we shall have the dictatorship of General Weygand."[15] Such bullying was not mere rhetoric. When the National Assembly met at the Vichy casino to take its fateful vote on the afternoon of 10 July, Vincent Badie, a Radical deputy, attempted to climb the podium to submit an alternative motion to Laval's, but ushers blocked his path and threw him "unceremoniously to the foot of the staircase."[16] Laval's words of menace, moreover, sharp and authoritarian in tone as they were, were constrained compared to the shrillness and bluster of his followers.

At a time of defeat and dislocation, with a number of the Chamber's most stalwart members absent or detained, with the Germans at hand and Pétain and Weygand in charge, it would have taken a brave soul to stand up to the arm-twisting of Laval and his minions. One hundred men had the wherewithal to do so, voting no or abstaining on 10 July.

Some will no doubt find such a summing-up too indulgent. There were mitigating circumstances, it might be conceded, but the fundamental fact remains: a crushing majority of the Republic's parliamentarians did cast the fatal ballots in the end. What more proof is needed of the bankruptcy of the regime's political class?

The failings of France's political class were of profound consequence, but it is worth pointing out that they were also momentary. No doubt not a single "prominent" politician rallied to de Gaulle in June 1940, and it is equally true that a full third of the old political class continued to back Vichy into 1942.[17] At the same time, an estimated one parliamentarian in six opposed the National Revolution from the outset (a contingent made up of the noes and abstentionists of 10 July, rounded out by a bloc of deputies and senators who had not been present to cast a ballot but remained staunch in their republican convictions). That proportion, moreover, would begin to grow from 1941, swelling to two out of three over the course of the year following and continuing to edge up thereafter as one-time Vichy backers, whether motivated by a new-found moral clarity or by simple opportunism, began to peel away. The Republic's political class, as the leading historian of the subject has put it, "came to its senses," not soon enough or in sufficient quantity to redeem itself, but enough to dispel accusations of unworthiness.[18]

The point is not to whitewash the old Republic. Reynaud made bad choices, and the National Assembly made a worse one, but that is just half the story. There were political forces dead set on democracy's demise, and they were ready to threaten, to criminalize, and to arrest in order to get the authoritarian outcome they desired. An alliance of army brass and senior civil servants worked together to push Reynaud out and bring Pétain in. An unscrupulous alliance of *mous* and right-wingers then finished off the job, harrying the National Assembly into an act of self-destruction. The Republic in 1940 was done in by its weaknesses, no doubt, but above all by its enemies.

At the highwater mark of Hitler's European imperium, democratic institutions had been wiped off the map everywhere on the continent, save in Finland, Sweden, and Switzerland. In this regard, the Third Republic's undoing was not a unique development; indeed, the regime lasted longer and put up more of a fight than just about any other form of government until the Soviet Union, no democratic paragon, got into the war. Also, had France held the line against Hitler's armies, which was not beyond the realm of possibility, the Republic would have held too. No defeat, no Vichy, and as I have tried to argue above, France's defeat was not decided in advance. As for Vichy itself, it was the work in the first instance of elites, military and civilian, with long-standing ambivalences about the legitimacy and effectiveness of parliamentary government. They had a counter-project in mind, and Hitler, anxious for peace and tranquility on Germany's southern flank, was willing to let them have a try. The final push was given by Laval, backed in turn by a coalition of right-wingers and appeasers at any price. Right-wing deputies with an animus against the Republic were not a novel presence on the French political scene, but the upheavals of the Depression decade—the street riots, the Blum experiment, and the attractions of authoritarian examples abroad—had toughened them and multiplied their number. As for the *mous*, they *were* something new. These one-time republicans had turned on a regime they once supported, haunted by the bloodletting of the Great War and driven mad by the specter of communist subversion. That Laval was able to muster so large a faction, that as many parliamentarians as did stood by Vichy up to 1942 and even beyond, is testimony to the corroding effects of the politics of the 1930s. By this measure, the regime was eaten away from within.

But make no mistake about the point at issue. It's not that France's fractious politics set the nation up for defeat on the battlefield but, rather, that they played into the hands of anti-regime elites once the battlefield disaster, like some slow-motion nightmare in Robert Paxton's celebrated phrase, was underway.[19] Most of the nation's representatives in fact came round once the nightmare of 1940 had passed, and anyhow it wasn't Laval, the politico, who leveraged the Reynaud administration out of power. He delivered the *coup de grâce* to an expiring Republic, but it was Pétain and Weygand, Baudouin and Bouthillier, who formed the execution squad that fired off the fatal volley. In this measure, it was not decadence or even a decadent parliamentarism that did in the Republic, but a betrayal, and it wasn't politicians who were the main culprits so much as military men and senior civil servants. They had never felt much attachment to democracy in whatever form, and the defeat gave them the chance to steer France into authoritarian waters, a change of course they believed essential to the nation's survival and rebirth.

THE 1940 SYNDROME[1]

Such a conclusion raises some obvious questions. If the decadence story is so far off the mark, why has it had such a long and popular run? And presuming the alternative narrative sketched in here, which lays overwhelming blame for the defeat on France's army brass, has some measure of validity, how does French history writ large—and not just 1940—look different?

In answer to the first question, the Republic's failings were admittedly real enough. France took its time grasping the seriousness of the Nazi threat and mustering a response. The response itself was not all that might have been hoped for, although it made sense for a democracy with a green, conscript army to work with and a public consciousness weighed down by painful and unhealed memories of the

Great War. Then in the face of defeat, the Republic failed again. Reynaud deserves credit for exploring all the possible alternatives to capitulation, but he did not have the decisiveness to follow through on any one of them. In the meantime, he populated his cabinet with the Republic's enemies, building up the pressure in favor of an armistice, just the course of action he most opposed. As for the National Assembly, whatever excuses may be made on its behalf, it still cast the decisive vote that mothballed the Republic and cleared the way for Vichy.

What has been argued here is not that a view critical of the Republic is without foundation, but that it is just one piece of the puzzle and not the most important one at that. What about the Germans, first of all? There was nothing predetermined in Hitler's decision to attack through the Ardennes, nor in Guderian's to disobey orders and race westward once French lines had been breached. German victory, and by extension French defeat, was a contingent event, almost as much a surprise to the victors as it was to the defeated.[2] With defeat looming, France's anti-republican elites swung into action, using every tactic fair and foul to get their way. It's not that they conspired, but that they soldiered toward a common goal because guided by a common *Weltanschauung*. The Weygands and Baudouins thought of themselves as true patriots, truer in their patriotism indeed than the parliamentarians who, they were convinced, had got France into its present predicament. What their beloved country needed first and foremost was a bracing dose of authority to lead the nation out of the slough of parliamentary democracy toward a more disciplined future.

It's impossible to understand the Republic's fate without factoring in the contributions of its adversaries, both foreign and homegrown. Not just that: when the Republic's record is scrutinized in comparative perspective, what it did manage to accomplish doesn't look so meager after all. The Low Countries, the English-speaking peoples, the Soviet Union, none of them were any better prepared for Hitler's attacks, nor did any of them perform better on the battlefield in the war's early stages (the Battle of Britain apart). In fact, they had all bet on France to do the heavy lifting, hoping to spare themselves the effort, and were caught short when things did not turn out as they hoped. If a judgment needs to be made, then it is not so much France that should stand accused but all those other countries who imagined France as their own first line of defense.

So, the declinist narrative, while off the mark in the main, is not altogether so. It has a measure of plausibility and, of even greater importance, it is a narrative with political uses. The point is an obvious one when applied to Vichy: Pétain's regime was among the first to speak of the rottenness of the Republic, all the better to legitimate its own project of national regeneration.

There were elements of the Resistance, moreover, that thought in similar terms, though without the same anti-republican animus. De Gaulle himself understood the nation's recent history in a decline-and-renewal frame-work.[3] Interwar France had lost its way, bogged down in parliamentary bickering on the home front while opting for stasis over change in military matters. Vichy was not the answer to France's ills but the ultimate expression of them, and renewal began not with the Marshal but with de Gaulle's radio appeal on 18 June, which called on the French to continue the fight. In the Gaullist scheme of things, France did just that, rallying to the general as a nation—all but, in the famous phrase, "a handful of *misérables*." Not every *résistant*, of course, subscribed to the Gaullist view, but it was the common coin of Resistance discourse to understand the anti-German struggle itself, with or without the general at the center, as a turning point. Taking up arms against Nazi barbarism was a puri-fying experience that elevated the Resistance militant above the petty partisanship of the old Republic. In the white heat of the anti-fascist struggle, a new elite was forged with the moral rigor and sense of purpose to effect a genuine revolution out of which a new France, built on self-sacrifice rather than on self-indulgence, might be born. Technocrats in Resistance ranks emphasized less the ethical than the economic possibilities of the situation. The backward Third Republic had failed to find a solution to the Depression and so left France unprepared for war against an enemy armed with the most advanced weaponry. The nation had foundered as a result, but a concerted program of economic modernization might yet turn things around, placing France once more in the European vanguard where it belonged.

The Resistance generated multiple, often overlapping projects—national, ethical, economic—but however varied, all were cast in a common mold. The Republic had failed; Vichy was even worse (although it took more than one *résistant* time to figure this out); but the war experience had swept away the detritus of the past, making possible a fresh start at the zero hour of the Liberation.

Not least of all, the Resistance's take on France's strange defeat found an early and unsurpassingly eloquent spokesman in Marc Bloch. Bloch's eyewitness testimony, unsparing in its dissection of France's shortcomings not just on the battlefield but as a society, gave singular credence to the declinist line of analysis. He was not after all just anyone, but a historian's historian, one of the profession's greats, and when he wrote of the demands of citizenship these were not idle words. Bloch was a first-hour *résistant* who went to a hero's death in front of a

German firing squad. What he had to say carried added weight because of the way he lived and died.

More than one political family, then, had a deep investment in the decadence narrative. There was good evidence to back it up, and the story, told both well and often, lent validity to a varied range of agendas. It's little wonder that it proved so durable.

But the make-up of France's political scene has undergone a sea change in the last half century. The events of 1968 and the general's death two years later have taken the sheen off the Gaullist project. There was, of course, no revolution at the Liberation. Moreover, the myth of revolution itself has taken some blows in recent decades with the collapse of the Soviet bloc and a pair of Mitterrand presidencies that proved nothing so much as that the Parti Socialiste was a governing party much like any other. As for the modernizers and technocrats, their faith in state-managed growth has come under heavy fire in the wake of the 1970s recession and the neo-liberal surge that followed. It's not that there is no future for Gaullism, the revolutionary idea, or technocracy in contemporary France, not at all. It's just that they no longer have the same aura of old. So too the stories that Gaullists, revolutionaries, and technocrats told about themselves, which, as we have seen, often took the decadence of the Third Republic (and even of the Fourth) as a point of departure.

The fading of once-dominant narratives—though not as told by Bloch whose account continues to occupy a special place of reverence—has cleared space for a different way of looking at the Third Republic's demise, and the contours of such a new understanding have been outlined in the pages preceding. Does France's history look different as a result?

In several ways, it does. First of all, France's 1930s look a little less dismal. There was always the bright spot of the Popular Front, but it now looks like the Daladier years that followed have something to be said for them as well.[4] France did not fail to prepare for war. It may have not been as ready as it could have been, but it was ready enough and more ready than most.

Then there is the question of how France under Vichy is itself to be looked at. An old, heroic view—that France was a nation of *résistants*—now lies in a heap, battered down by a series of counter-arguments. Pétain's National Revolution did not come out of nowhere but had roots deep in French soil; the Marshal himself was a popular figure and remained so until the end; and the Resistance, however much it grew over the course of the Occupation, never encompassed the nation as a whole.

But if the French weren't resisters, what were they? Recent literature has spotlighted not so much the French public's enduring Pétainism as its basic indifference to politics. The Occupation was hard, and in the midst of material want and unheated winters most people worried about how to find food and coal, not about Vichy policy.

Yet there may be another way of thinking about all this. The defeat and the exodus were disorienting, no doubt, but there is reason to believe that the disorientation did not last long. Vichy tried to use the loss of life at Mers el-Kebir to stoke anti-British sentiment, but public opinion did not buy the regime's line. Prefectural reports noted the public's admiration for British steadfastness during the Battle of Britain, and that admiration did not flag.[5] The onset of food shortages, accompanied by a rash of rationing scandals, in the winter of 1940–1 ate deeper into the Vichy regime's prestige and support.

Now, the public did not balk when Vichy enacted anti-Semitic legislation in the fall of 1940, but it did in reaction to the round-up of Jews a year and a half later. In July 1942 the regime under German pressure undertook the arrest of 12,000 Parisian Jews, who were interned first in the Vélodrome d'hiver before eventual deportation to Reich territory. The event was met with general reproof, amplified by the protests of a number of senior Catholic clergy. The protests, it might be added, were not just behind-the-scenes gestures but in many instances vocal declarations read from the pulpit. The Church hierarchy might align itself with Pétain on many things but not on its complicity in the implementation of the Occupier's program of mass arrests and deportations. This is not to say that anti-Semitism was a negligible quantity in Vichy-era France—far from it—just that when push came to shove there were moral limits that many French were not willing to cross.[6]

In all, 1942 proved a disastrous year for the regime's standing with the public. The trouble began in February/March with the bungled management of the Riom trials, which created sympathy for the defendants, Blum and Daladier among them. It ended in November with the German occupation of the southern zone in the wake of the Allies' successful invasion of North Africa, proof positive of Vichy's inability to protect French national sovereignty. In case further evidence was needed of the regime's abjection, it imposed a labor draft in February 1943 (the Service du travail obligatoire) at the behest of the Germans who were ravenous for manpower. Vichy implicated itself in the process and—to its utter discredit—in the sacrifice of the nation's youth to the Moloch of the Nazi war machine. The French may have turned to Vichy in desperation in July 1940, but within a year or two at the most they had turned away again.[7]

This trajectory has implications for how the Resistance itself is to be evaluated. Conceived of as an organized movement engaged in a range of clandestine activities,

CONCLUSION

from propaganda work to intelligence gathering to armed struggle, it was indeed a minority affair. No doubt, in comparative terms, it was one of the largest and most unified of its kind in Europe, but, taking numbers alone into account, it mobilized no more than a hard-core elite, an estimated 2 percent or so of the national population. In recent years, however, a different way of understanding the Resistance has been proposed, focused less on organization—on movements and networks—than on what has been called "the civil Resistance." The term encompasses a range of illegal activities: helping out downed Allied aviators, harboring persecuted Jews, abetting labor draft dodgers. The objective may not have been the overthrow of Vichy or the ejection of the German occupier, but enormous personal risks were involved nonetheless. When added together, it has been argued, such individual and small-group efforts, a "cloud of gestures" as one historian has labeled them, constituted a veritable "society of rescue." This society in turn provided an indispensable medium, sympathetic and supportive, that enabled the movements and networks of the regular Resistance to do their work. It was the ocean in which the fish of the armed Resistance swam, to rephrase Mao's celebrated dictum. Looked at in this way, the Resistance was indeed a mass phenomenon.[8]

A final point has to do with the ideological glue that held it all together, a public less and less enamored of

162

Vichy and a Resistance movement, both armed and civil, that was on the rise. Writing in 1942, the novelist Irène Nemirovsky reflected on the tidal flows of public opinion, its abandonment first of the Republic and then of Vichy: "The French grew tired of the Republic as if she were an old wife. For them, the dictatorship was a brief affair, adultery. But they intended to cheat on their wife, not to kill her. Now they realize that she is dead, their Republic, their freedom. They are mourning her."[9] It's too simple to think of the French, having recovered from the shocks of defeat and exodus, as once again republicans one and all, but Nemirovsky's remarks are a reminder that the idea of the Republic still carried weight. De Gaulle himself was well aware of this. As a military man, the symbolism of republican tradition may not have meant that much, but from 1941 he had ever more recourse to it. At the outset, Free France had campaigned under the military motto, "Honor and Fatherland," but to that slogan was soon added a new (or, rather, not so new) one, the venerable trio of "Liberty, Equality, Fraternity." As the interior Resistance ramified, de Gaulle pushed the various movements to unify, a policy that resulted in the formation of the Conseil national de la Résistance in May 1943. The general insisted further, and to the chagrin of many *résistants* looking for a sharp break with the past, that the body include representatives of France's old parties. He pursued a similar course of action in liberated Algiers when constituting a consultative assembly, what amounted to a parliament in exile. The assembly was created in September that same year, former deputies and senators of the defunct Third Republic accounting for a full quarter of its membership.[10] De Gaulle's motives were no doubt multiple. He wanted to show the Anglo-Americans that he was a democrat who deserved respect. He wanted to show self-styled Giraudistes that France stood behind him and not Giraud. But he was also expressing recognition that the French, however at sea in 1940, had in due course recovered their republican moorings. Republican slogans, institutions, and even personnel still mattered to them, and now they mattered to de Gaulle too, who so deeply aspired to incarnate the national spirit.

It is important to strike the right balance here. France was not a nation of *attentistes* preoccupied with hunting up the next meal while waiting to see how the war played out, but neither was it a nation of resisters. There remained right down to the end a minoritarian current loyal to the National Revolution and a greater number still who continued to have faith in the Marshal. On the other side of the ledger, however, the Resistance phenomenon was larger than recent literature intent on debunking Gaullist myths concedes, and it fed off of popular sympathies that deepened with every passing month. There was a moral reawakening over the course of the Occupation, and it took place under the sign of the Republic, of a political form—republican democracy—that had once seemed discredited.

No doubt such a claim is more speculative than proven, but it does help to make sense of a puzzling fact. The Fourth Republic, in constitution and parliamentary modus operandi, bore a striking resemblance to the Third. There were critical differences: the executive branch was endowed with welfare and planning authority it had never had before; Christian Democrats and Communists were numerous in a way they had not been in the 1930s. In many respects, though, there were continuities, enough so that many *résistants* who had nurtured dreams of a revolutionary transformation wrote in plaintive tones of a "restoration." The term is exaggerated, but I do think it is fair to speak of an enduring, public commitment to republican values and institutions that was interrupted by the defeat and the exodus but that reknit itself, like a broken bone, in the first years of the Occupation.

Think of the 1940 defeat as a military event and not as an expression of national decline, and then certain features of the war and post-war scene become that much easier to account for: the public's rapid disenchantment with Vichy, the expansion of the Resistance understood in broadest terms, and over all the staying power of the republican idea. Vichy for all that does not become a parenthesis in French history. It drew on long-standing currents of anti-republican feeling, swelled by the crisis of the 1930s; it maintained a constituency right down to the end; and it left a significant policy legacy behind. Yet, even if the regime enjoyed a majoritarian moment in the summer of 1940, that moment did not last long. There were popular constituencies to which the regime appealed—nationalist, Catholic, fascist—but their numbers dwindled in time, and on the whole it was among the nation's elites, rather than the public at large, that the regime found its most kindred spirits.

In recent decades, there has been a revival of interest in France's republican tradition, a tradition that, as argued here, had more tenacity, even in the darkest of moments, than sometimes thought. In the 1930s the Republic looked like an also-ran in a race dominated by fascists and communists. In the 1940s and 1950s it was hobbled by a stubborn attachment to empire that spawned decades of grisly colonial warfare. But now that the Cold War is over and the imperial era has closed, the republican idea looks a good deal more appealing. The search for an alternative path has lost urgency, and the most pressing question now is what kind of Republic the French want. It is a question as pertinent to citizens of sister Republics as it is to the French themselves.

NOTES

Introduction: Strange Defeat?

1. Guderian cited in Karl-Heinz Frieser, *Blitzkrieg-Legende: der Westfeldzug 1940* (Munich, 1995), 3.
2. Philippe Pétain, *Actes et écrits* (Paris, 1974), 450.
3. Marc Bloch, *Strange Defeat: A Statement of Evidence Written in 1940*, tr. Gerard Hopkins (New York, 1968).
4. Stanley Hoffmann et al., *In Search of France: The Economy, Society, and Political System of the Twentieth Century* (New York, 1965; orig. 1963).
5. Jean-Baptiste Duroselle, "Changes in French Foreign Policy since 1945," in Hoffmann et al., *In Search of France*, 318; idem, *La Décadence, 1932–1939* (Paris, 1979).
6. William L. Shirer, *The Collapse of the Third Republic: An Inquiry into the Fall of France in 1940* (New York, 1969); Alistair Horne, *To Lose a Battle: France 1940* (Boston, MA, 1969).
7. John C. Cairns, "Some Recent Historians and the 'Strange Defeat' of 1940," *Journal of Modern History*, 46 (March 1974), 60–85; Robert J. Young, *In Command of France: French Foreign Policy and Military Planning, 1933–1940* (Cambridge, MA, 1978); William D. Irvine, "Domestic Politics and the Fall of France in 1940," in Joel Blatt, ed., *The French Defeat of 1940: Reassessments* (New York, 1998), 85–99; Ernest R. May, *Strange Victory: Hitler's Conquest of France* (New York, 2000); Julian Jackson, *The Fall of France: The Nazi Invasion of 1940* (Oxford, 2003). The French have also taken a fresh look at the subject. See Jean-Louis Crémieux-Brilhac, *Les Français de l'an 40* (Paris, 1990), 2 vols.

Chapter 1: Diplomacy

1. Jean Doise and Maurice Vaïsse, *Diplomatie et outil militaire, 1871–1991* (Paris, 1992), 398.
2. Ibid, 368.
3. Julian Jackson, *The Fall of France: The Nazi Invasion of 1940* (Oxford, 2003), 77; Jeffrey A. Gunsburg, *Divided and Conquered: The French High Command and the Defeat of the West, 1940* (Westport, CT, 1979), 77.
4. The toughest critics are the French themselves, starting with Jean-Baptiste Duroselle, but historians of Eastern Europe are not far behind: Piotr Wandycz, *The Twilight of French Eastern Alliances, 1926–1936: French-Czechoslovak–Polish Relations from Locarno to the Remilitarization of the Rhineland* (Princeton, NJ, 1988); Nicole Jordan, *The Popular Front and Central Europe: The Dilemmas of French Impotence, 1918–1940* (Cambridge, 1992); Michael J. Carley, *1939: The Alliance that Never Was and the Coming of World War II* (Chicago, IL, 1999).
5. For a good summary of France's Locarno policy, see Wandycz, *The Twilight of French Eastern Alliances*, ch. 1. See also Peter Jackson, "French Security and a British 'Continental Commitment' after the First World War: A Reassessment," *European Historical Review*, 126 (April 2011), 383.
6. P. M. H. Bell, *France and Britain 1900–1940: Entente and Estrangement* (London, 1996), 186–8.
7. Martin S. Alexander, *The Republic in Danger: General Maurice Gamelin and the Politics of French Defence, 1933–1940* (Cambridge, 1992), 188–90.
8. Gunsburg, *Divided and Conquered*, 30–1; Martin Thomas, *Britain, France and Appeasement: Anglo-French Relations in the Popular Front Era* (Oxford, 1996), 30–4; Bell, *France and Britain*, 205–6; Anthony Adamthwaite, *France and the Coming of the Second World War, 1936–1939* (London, 1977), 37–9.
9. William Shirer, *The Collapse of the Third Republic: An Inquiry into the Fall of France in 1940* (New York, 1994; orig. 1969), 247.
10. Adamthwaite, *Grandeur and Misery: France's Bid for Power in Europe, 1914–1940* (London, 1995), 204.
11. Robert Frankenstein, "The Decline of France and French Appeasement Policies, 1936–9," in Wolfgang J. Mommsen and Lothar Kettenacker, eds, *The Fascist Challenge and the Policy of Appeasement* (London, 1983), 241.
12. Cited in Robert O. Paxton, *Europe in the Twentieth Century* (New York, 1975), 419.
13. The exchange of views is recounted in Shirer, *The Collapse of the Third Republic*, 330–40.
14. Gunsberg, *Divided and Conquered*, 66–7.
15. David Reynolds, *From Munich to Pearl Harbor: Roosevelt's America and the Origins of the Second World War* (Chicago, IL, 2001), 47; Frankenstein, "The Decline of France and French Appeasement Policies," 243.
16. Adamthwaite, "France and the Coming of War," in Mommsen and Kettenacker, eds, *The Fascist Challenge and the Policy of Appeasement*, 250;

Adamthwaite, *France and the Coming of the Second World War*, 252–3; Daniel Hucker, *Public Opinion and the End of Appeasement in Britain and France* (Farnham, 2011), 63–4; Talbot C. Imlay, "France, Britain and the Making of the Anglo-French Alliance, 1938–39," in Martin S. Alexander and William J. Philpott, eds, *Anglo-French Defence Relations between the Wars* (Basingstoke, 2002), 93.

17. Robert A. Doughty, "The Illusion of Security: France, 1919–1940," in Williamson Murray, MacGregor Knox, and Alvin Bernstein, eds, *The Making of Strategy: Rulers, States and War* (Cambridge, 1994), 487–8.
18. Adamthwaite, *Grandeur and Misery*, 222.
19. Carley is insistent on this point. See Carley, "Prelude to Defeat: Franco-Soviet Relations, 1919–1939," in Joel Blatt, ed., *The French Defeat: Reassessments* (New York, 1998), 171–203.
20. Bell, *France and Britain*, 224–5; Adamthwaite, *France and the Coming of the Second World War*, 49–50; Robert J. Young, *France and the Origins of the Second World War* (London, 1996), 126.
21. Wandycz, *The Twilight of French Eastern Alliances*, 323.
22. Richard Overy, *1939: Countdown to War* (London, 2009), 13.
23. For a general assessment of Great Britain's diplomatic *Weltanschauung*, see Paul Kennedy, "The Tradition of Appeasement in British Foreign Policy, 1865–1939," idem, ed., *Strategy and Diplomacy: 1870–1945* (London, 1983), 15–39; Bell, *France and Britain*, 178–9, 182, 223; Williamson Murray, "Britain," in Robert Boyce and Joseph A. Maiolo, eds, *The Origins of World War Two: The Debate Continues* (Basingstoke, 2003), 123–4; and Brian Bond, "The Continental Commitment in British Strategy in the 1930s," in Mommsen and Kettenacker, eds, *The Fascist Challenge and the Policy of Appeasement*, 197–201.
24. Reynolds, *From Munich to Pearl Harbor*, 31–2, 66.
25. Ibid, passim.
26. Sylvio Pons, *Stalin and the Inevitable War: 1936–1941* (London, 2002), 179–81.
27. Geoffrey Roberts, *Stalin's Wars: From World War to Cold War, 1939–1953* (New Haven, CT, 2006), 61–4.
28. Gabriel Gorodetsky, *Grand Delusion: Stalin and the German Invasion of Russia* (New Haven, CT, 1999), 279, 298–9.
29. Peter Jackson, "France," in Boyce and Maiolo, eds, *The Origins of World War Two*, 104.

Chapter 2: Armaments and Morale

1. Jean-Louis Crémieux-Brilhac, *Les Français de l'an 40* (Paris, 1990), vol. I, 17.
2. John Cairns, "Planning for *la guerre des masses*: Constraints and Contradictions in France before 1940," in Harry R. Borowski, ed., *Military Planning in the Twentieth Century* (Washington, DC, 1986), 41; Jean Doise and Maurice Vaïsse, *Diplomatie et outil militaire, 1871–1991*

(Paris, 1992), 349–50; Eugenia C. Kiesling, *Arming against Hitler: France and the Limits of Planning* (Lawrence, KS, 1996), 171.

3. Adam Tooze, *The Wages of Destruction: The Making and Breaking of the Nazi Economy* (London, 2006), 65.

4. Robert Frankenstein, *Le Prix du réarmement français (1935–1939)* (Paris, 1982), 33; Julian Jackson, *The Fall of France: The Nazi Invasion of 1940* (Oxford, 2003), 13.

5. See Herrick Chapman, *State Capitalism and Working-Class Radicalism in the French Aircraft Industry* (Berkeley and Los Angeles, CA, 1991), Part II.

6. Frankenstein, *Le Prix du réarmement*, 71, 74, 86, 91.

7. Crémieux-Brilhac, *Les Français de l'an 40*, vol. II, 167–8; Robert A. Doughty, *The Seeds of Disaster: The Development of French Army Doctrine, 1919–1939* (Hamden, CT, 1985), 183.

8. Frank[enstein], *La Hantise du déclin. Le rang de la France en Europe, 1920–1960: finances, défense et identité nationale* (Paris, 1994), 49.

9. Doise and Vaïsse, *Diplomatie et outil militaire*, 402, 404; Crémieux-Brilhac, *Les Français de l'an 40*, vol. I, 129.

10. Doise and Vaïsse, *Diplomatie et outil militaire*, 402; Frankenstein, *Le Prix du réarmement*, 34–5; Robert J. Young, *France and the Origins of the Second World War* (London, 1996), 122.

11. Jeffrey A. Gunsberg, *Divided and Conquered: The French High Command and the Defeat of the West, 1940* (Westport, CT, 1979), 16; Martin S. Alexander, *The Republic in Danger: General Maurice Gamelin and the Politics of French Defeat, 1933–1940* (Cambridge, 1992), 166; Crémieux-Brilhac, *Les Français de l'an 40*, vol. II, 55–6.

12. Crémieux-Brilhac, *Les Français de l'an 40*, vol. II, 27; Frankenstein, *Le Prix du réarmement*, 189; Frank[enstein], *Hantise du déclin*, 45.

13. For the first line of criticism, see Doise and Vaïsse, *Diplomatie et outil militaire*, 387, 398; for the second, see Talbot C. Imlay, *Facing the Second World War: Strategy, Politics, and Economics in Britain and France 1938–1940* (Oxford, 2003), passim.

14. Sylvio Pons, *Stalin and the Inevitable War: 1936–1941* (London, 2002), 194; Gabriel Gorodetsky, *Grand Delusion: Stalin and the German Invasion of Russia* (New Haven, CT, 1999), 115.

15. Geoffrey Roberts, *Stalin's Wars: From World War to Cold War, 1939–1953* (New Haven, CT, 2006), 16.

16. Gorodetsky, *Grand Delusion*, 241, 243; Roberts, *Stalin's Wars*, 54.

17. David Reynolds, *From Munich to Pearl Harbor: Roosevelt's America and the Origins of the Second World War* (Chicago, IL, 2001), 78; Waldo Heinrichs, *Threshold of War: Franklin D. Roosevelt and American Entry into World War II* (New York, 1988), 160.

18. Heinrichs, *Threshold of War*, 8, 10; Reynolds, *From Munich to Pearl Harbor*, 115.

19. Heinrichs, *Threshold of War*, 10–11; Reynolds, *From Munich to Pearl Harbor*, 115.

20. Heinrichs, *Threshold of War*, 67, 183.
21. Tooze, *The Wages of Destruction*, 176, 454; Richard Overy, *Why the Allies Won* (New York, 1997).
22. Tooze, *Wages of Destruction*, 65, 164, 315.
23. The phrase is Klaus Hildebrand's, as cited in Crémieux-Brilhac, *Les Français de l'an 40*, vol. II, 347.
24. Tooze, *Wages of Destruction*, 304, 315, 317, 321, 328–9.
25. Doughty, *Seeds of Disaster*, 2; Anthony Adamthwaite, *France and the Coming of the Second World War, 1936–1939* (London, 1977), 358; Cairns, "Along the Road Back to France 1940," *American Historical Review*, 64 (April 1959), 601.
26. G. C. Peden, *British Rearmament and the Treasury, 1932–1939* (Edinburgh, 1979), 1–2, 10, 184.
27. Imlay, *Facing the Second World War*, 14–15.
28. Crémieux-Brilhac, *Les Français de l'an 40*, vol. II, 132, 351.
29. Andrew Shennan, *The Fall of France, 1940* (London, 2000), 136; Pierre Laborie, *L'Opinion française sous Vichy* (Paris, 1990), 55; Imlay, *Facing the Second World War*, 26.
30. L'Herbier cited in Jean Bertin-Maghit, *Le Cinéma français sous l'Occupation* (Paris, 1994), 31.
31. Crémieux-Brilhac, *Les Français de l'an 40*, vol. I, 62–5; William D. Irvine, "Domestic Politics and the Fall of France in 1940," in Joel Blatt, ed., *The French Defeat of 1940: Reassessments* (New York, 2006), 95.
32. Crémieux-Brilhac, *Les Français de l'an 40*, vol. I, 62; Young, *France and the Origins of the Second World War*, 33. See also Jessica Wardhaugh, *In Pursuit of the People: Political Culture in France, 1934–39* (London, 2009), 217–25.
33. Reynolds, *From Munich to Pearl Harbor*, 92–3, 98.
34. Paul Kennedy, "The Tradition of Appeasement in British Foreign Policy, 1865–1939," in Kennedy, ed., *Strategy and Diplomacy: 1870–1945* (London, 1983), 36.
35. Julian Jackson, "Etrange défaite française ou étrange victoire anglaise?," in Maurice Vaïsse, ed., *Mai–juin 1940: Défaite française, victoire allemande, sous l'oeil des historiens étrangers* (Paris, 2000), 177–213.
36. Roberts, *Stalin's Wars*, 19.
37. Ernest May, *Strange Victory: Hitler's Conquest of France* (New York, 2000), 83, 92, 215, 221; Karl-Heinz Frieser, *Blitzkrieg Legende: Des Westfeldzug 1940* (Munich, 1995), 69; Donald Cameron Watt, *Too Serious a Business: European Armed Forces and the Approach of the Second World War* (Berkeley and Los Angeles, CA, 1975), 144; Jackson, "Etrange défaite française ou étrange victoire anglaise?," 185.

Chapter 3: Battle Plans

1. Marc Bloch, *Strange Defeat: A Statement of Evidence Written in 1940*, tr. Gerard Hopkins (New York, 1968), 36, 52–3.

2. Nicole Jordan, "Strategy and Scapegoatism: Reflections on the French National Catastrophe, 1940," in Joel Blatt, ed., *The French Defeat of 1940: Reassessments* (New York, 2006), 18, 21.

3. Jean-Louis Crémieux-Brilhac, *Les Français de l'an 40* (Paris, 1990), vol. II, 378.

4. Alistair Horne, *To Lose a Battle: France 1940* (Boston, MA, 1969), passim.

5. Robert A. Doughty, *The Seeds of Disaster: The Development of French Army Doctrine, 1919–1939* (Hamden, CT, 1985), 69–70.

6. Ibid, 59–60, 70–1.

7. Ibid, 90–1, 111.

8. Jeffrey A. Gunsburg, *Divided and Conquered: The French High Command and the Defeat of the West, 1940* (Westport, CT, 1979), 268.

9. Ernest May, *Strange Victory: Hitler's Conquest of France* (New York, 2000), 402–3; Gunsburg, *Divided and Conquered*, 209–10; Karl-Heinz Frieser, *Blitzkrieg-Legende: Der Westfeldzug 1940* (Munich, 1995), 302–3.

10. This is very close to the argument advanced in Eugenia C. Kiesling, *Arming against Hitler: France and the Limits of Military Planning* (Lawrence, KS, 1996), 118, 171.

11. Martin S. Alexander, *The Republic in Danger: General Maurice Gamelin and the Politics of French Defence, 1933–1940* (Cambridge, 1992), 269–70.

12. John Keegan, *Six Armies in Normandy* (London, 1994), 41–6.

13. Geoffrey Roberts, *Stalin's Wars: From World War to Cold War, 1939–1953* (New Haven, CT, 2006), 67, 69–70, 79–80; Gabriel Gorodetsky, *Grand Delusion: Stalin and the German Invasion of Russia* (New Haven, CT, 1999), 126–30, 241–2, 319.

14. Russell Weigley, *The American Way of War: A History of United States Military Strategy and Policy* (New York, 1973).

15. Max Hastings, *Inferno: The World at War, 1939–1945* (New York, 2011), passim.

16. See Robert Frank[enstein], *La Hantise du déclin. Le Rang de la France, 1920–1960: finances, défense et identité nationale* (Paris, 1994), 92–3.

17. Talbot C. Imlay, "Paul Reynaud and France's Response to Nazi Germany, 1938–1940," *French Historical Studies*, 26 (Summer 2003), 527–30.

18. May, *Strange Victory*, 6.

19. Frieser, *Blitzkrieg-Legende*, 18.

20. Adam Tooze, *The Wages of Destruction: The Making and Breaking of the Nazi Economy* (London, 2006), 328–9.

21. Robert Frankenstein, *Le Prix du réarmement français (1935–1939)* (Paris, 1982), 269; and Frank[enstein], "The Second World War through French and British Eyes," in Robert Tombs and Emile Chabal, eds, *Britain and France in Two World Wars: Truth, Myth and Memory* (London, 2013), 181.

22. Crémieux-Brilhac, *Les Français de l'an 40*, vol. I, 410; vol. II, 365.

23. Gerhard L. Weinberg, *A World at Arms: A Global History of World War II* (Cambridge, 2005), 111.

24. Frieser, *Blitzkrieg-Legende*, 71–82, 91, 111; May, *Strange Victory*, 236.
25. Tooze, *Wages of Destruction*, 377.
26. Alexander, *Gamelin*, passim.
27. Don W. Alexander, "The Repercussions of the Breda Variant," *French Historical Studies*, 8 (Spring 1974), 478–84; Gunsburg, *Divided and Conquered*, 270; Doughty, "The Illusion of Security: France, 1919–1940," in Williamson Murray, MacGregor Knox, and Alvin Bernstein, eds, *The Making of Strategy: Rulers, States, and War* (Cambridge, 1994), 492–4.
28. Alexander, "The Repercussions of the Breda Variant," 484. See also Williamson Murray, "May, 1940: Contingency and Fragility of the German RMA," in MacGregor Knox and Williamson Murray, eds, *The Dynamics of Military Revolution, 1300–2050* (Cambridge, 2001), 164–5; Doughty, *Seeds of Disaster*, 67.

Chapter 4: Lightning War

1. Jeffrey A. Gunsburg, *Divided and Conquered: The French High Command and the Defeat of the West, 1940* (Westport, CT, 1979), 124–5; Nicole Jordan, "Strategy and Scapegoatism: Reflections on the French National Catastrophe, 1940," in Joel Blatt, ed., *The French Defeat of 1940: Reassessments* (New York, 2006), 26; Julian Jackson, *The Fall of France: The Nazi Invasion of 1940* (Oxford, 2003), 93.
2. Robert J. Young, *France and the Origins of the Second World War* (London, 1996), 142; Robert A. Doughty, *The Seeds of Disaster: The Development of French Army Doctrine, 1919–1939* (Hamden, CT, 1985), 2–3.
3. Alistair Horne, *To Lose a Battle: France 1940* (Boston, MA, 1969), 306.
4. Karl-Heinz Frieser, *Blitzkrieg-Legende: Der Westfeldzug 1940* (Munich, 1995), passim; on Guderian's insubordination, see idem, 242–3; Young, *France and the Origins of the Second World War*, 232; Gerhard L. Weinberg, *A World at Arms: A Global History of World War II* (Cambridge, 2005), 108–9.
5. Edward R. Hooten, *Luftwaffe at War: Blitzkrieg in the West, 1939–1940* (Hersham, 2007), vol. II, 61.
6. Jackson, *The Fall of France*, 47–8; Frieser, *Blitzkrieg-Legende*, 248–50.
7. Hoth, cited in Horne, *To Lose a Battle*, 355; Frieser, *Blitzkrieg-Legende*, 250–66.
8. Williamson Murray, "May, 1940: Contingency and Fragility of the German RMA," in MacGregor Knox and Williamson Murray, eds, *The Dynamics of Military Revolution, 1300–2050* (Cambridge, 2001), 172.
9. Gunsburg, *Divided and Conquered*, 248–50, 255–8, 265; Jackson, *The Fall of France*, 86–8.
10. Jackson, *The Fall of France*, 85–8.
11. Jean Doise and Maurice Vaïsse, *Diplomatie et outil militaire, 1871–1991* (Paris, 1992), 424–5; Doughty, *Seeds of Disaster*, 190; Weinberg, *A World at Arms*, 127.

12. Gunsburg, *Divided and Conquered*, 191.
13. On France's air war, see Patrick Facon, "L'Armée de l'air dans la bataille de 1940: mythes, légendes et réalités," in Christine Levisse-Touzé, ed., *La Campagne de 1940* (Paris, 2001), 216–19.
14. John C. Cairns, "Some Recent Historians and the 'Strange Defeat' of 1940," *Journal of Modern History*, 46 (March 1974), 79; Général Jean Delmas, "La Manoeuvre générale, surprise allemande, défense française," in Levisse-Touzé, ed., *La Campagne de 1940*, 124; Martin Alexander, "Dunkirk in Military Operations, Myths and Memories," in Robert Tombs and Emile Chabal, eds, *Britain and France in Two World Wars: Truth, Myth and Memory* (London, 2013), 96.
15. Gunsburg, *Divided and Conquered*, 266; Doughty, *Seeds of Disaster*, 190; P. M. H. Bell, *France and Britain 1900–1940: Entente and Estrangement* (London, 1996), 240–1; Jean-Louis Crémieux-Brilhac, *Les Français de l'an 40* (Paris, 1990), vol. II, 644, 648.
16. Colonel Jacques Vernet, "La Bataille de la Somme," in Levisse-Touzé, ed., *La Campagne de 1940*, 198–208; André Martel, "Conclusion générale," in ibid, 565.
17. Martel, "Conclusion générale," 557. But in the same volume Jean-Jacques Anzalier makes the case that the losses may have been a deal less severe. See Anzalier, "La Campagne de mai–juin 1940. Les pertes?," in Levisse-Touzé, ed., *La Campagne de 1940*, 442.
18. Charles de Gaulle, *The War Memoirs of Charles de Gaulle: The Call to Honour, 1940–1942*, tr. Jonathan Griffin (New York, 1955), 8; Tony Judt, "Could the French Have Won?," *New York Review of Books* (22 February 2001), 37–40.
19. David Reynolds, "Churchill and the British 'Decision' to Fight on in 1940: Right Policy, Wrong Reasons," in Richard Langhorne, ed., *Diplomacy and Intelligence during the Second World War: Essays in Honour of F. H. Hinsley* (Cambridge, 1985), 149–51; idem, "Churchill in 1940: The Worst and Finest Hour," in Robert Blake and William Roger Louis, eds, *Churchill* (New York, 1993), 248–9.

Chapter 5: Armistice

1. See Jean-Pierre Azéma, *1940: l'année terrible* (Paris, 1990), 207.
2. Olivier Wieviorka, *Les Orphelins de la République. Destinées des députés et sénateurs français (1940–1945)* (Paris, 2001), 53, 93, 97. This is by far the best book on the subject.
3. On Ybarnégaray, see William Irvine, *French Conservatism in Crisis: The Republican Federation of France in the 1930s* (Baton Rouge, LA, 1979), 14.
4. Paul Baudouin, *Neuf mois au gouvernement (avril–décembre 1940)* (Paris, 1948), 90–1.
5. On Weygand, see Philip Bankwitz, *Maxime Weygand and Civil-Military Relations in Modern France* (Cambridge, MA, 1967), 9, 183.

6. Charles de Gaulle, *The Complete War Memoirs of Charles de Gaulle: The Call to Honour, 1940–1942*, tr. Jonathan Griffin (New York, 1955), 55; Baudouin, *Neuf mois*, 89, 162.
7. Baudouin, *Neuf mois*, 122.
8. See Fred Kupferman, *Laval* (Paris, 1987), 244–5.
9. 24 May to be precise. See Baudouin, *Neuf mois*, 76, 91; and Jean-Louis Crémieux-Brilhac, *Les Français de l'an 40* (Paris, 1990), vol. I, 268.
10. Emmanuel Berl, *La Fin de la IIIe République* (Paris, 2007, orig. 1968), 87; Crémieux-Brilhac, *Les Français de l'an 40*, vol. I, 269.
11. Baudouin, *Neuf mois*, 133–6.
12. Ibid, 149.
13. P. M. H. Bell, *France and Britain 1900–1940: Entente and Estrangement* (London, 1996), 242–5; Hanna Diamond, *Fleeing Hitler: France 1940* (Oxford, 2007), 94–100.
14. Baudouin, *Neuf mois*, 149, 152, 162; Yves Bouthillier, *Le Drame de Vichy: face à l'ennemi, face à l'allié* (Paris, 1950), 68–70.
15. Baudouin, *Neuf mois*, 143–4, 165–6; Bouthillier, *Le Drame de Vichy*, 74.
16. Bouthillier, *Le Drame de Vichy*, 25, 73–87.
17. Crémieux-Brilhac, *Les Francçais de l'an 40*, vol. I, 597.
18. Historians have debated the North African option. Some have expressed doubts about its feasibility: see the discussion in Christine Levisse-Touzé, *L'Afrique du Nord dans la guerre, 1939–1945* (Paris, 1998), 81–4. But others have arrived at the opposite conclusion: Douglas Porch, "Arms and Alliances: French Grand Strategy and Policy in 1914 and 1940," in Paul Kennedy, ed., *Grand Strategies in War and Peace* (New Haven, CT, 1991), 132: and at greater length, Jacques Sapir, Frank Stora, and Loïc Mahé, *1940. Et si la France avait continué la guerre ... Essai d'alternative historique* (Paris, 2010), passim. In any event, the option was not tried.
19. Julian Jackson, *The Fall of France: The Nazi Invasion of 1940* (Oxford, 2003), 142; Bouthillier, *Le Drame de Vichy*, 75, 126.
20. Bankwitz, *Weygand*, 315, 318.
21. De Gaulle, *The Complete War Memoirs*, vol. I, 60–3.
22. Cited in Michèle and Jean-Paul Cointet, eds, *Dictionnaire historique de la France sous l'Occupation* (Paris, 2000), 375.
23. Crémieux-Brilhac, *Les Français de l'an 40*, vol. I, 605; see also Martin S. Alexander, *The Republic in Danger: General Maurice Gamelin and the Politics of French Defence, 1933–1940* (Cambridge, 1992), 2.
24. Robert O. Paxton, *Vichy France: Old Guard and New Order, 1940–1944* (New York, 1972), 268.

Chapter 6: The Road to Vichy

1. H. Roderick Kedward, "Patriots and Patriotism in Vichy France," *Transactions of the Royal Historical Society*, 32 (1982), 181; Jean-Pierre Rioux, "L'exode: un pays à la dérive," *Histoire*, 129 (January 1990), n.p.;

Nicole Dombrowski, *Beyond the Battlefield: The French Civilian Exodus of May–June 1940* (PhD dissertation, New York University, 1995), 514, 527; Hannah Diamond, *Fleeing Hitler: France 1940* (Oxford, 2007), 176.

2. The point is argued vigorously by Dombrowski, *Beyond the Battlefield*, 7, 317.
3. Joseph Paul-Boncour, cited in Diamond, *Fleeing Hitler*, 98.
4. Paul Baudouin, *Neuf mois au gouvernement (avril–décembre 1940)* (Paris, 1948), 224–5; see also 215–18.
5. Ibid., 195.
6. Jean-Louis Crémieux-Brilhac, *Les Français de l'an 40* (Paris, 1990), vol. I, 601.
7. Jean Montigny, *Toute la vérité sur un mois dramatique de notre histoire* (Clermont-Ferrand, 1970), 24–30; see also Fred Kupferman, *Laval* (Paris, 1987), 252.
8. Montigny, *Toute la vérité*, 24, 30–1.
9. Christine Levisse-Touzé, *L'Afrique du Nord dans la guerre 1939–1945* (Paris, 1998), 75.
10. Yves Bouthillier, *Le Drame de Vichy: face à l'ennemi, face à l'allié* (Paris, 1950), 107–9.
11. Philip Bankwitz, *Maxime Weygand and Civil-Military Relations in Modern France* (Cambridge, MA, 1967), 322.
12. Baudouin, *Neuf mois*, 229.
13. Crémieux-Brilhac, *Les Français de l'an 40*, vol. I, 620.
14. Blum speaking at Pétain's trial in 1945, cited in Kupferman, *Laval*, 259.
15. Montigny, *Toute la vérité*, 70–9; Kupferman, *Laval*, 264–7; Bankwitz, *Weygand*, 331.
16. Jean Sagnes, "Le refus républicain: les quatre-vingts parlementaires qui dirent 'non' à Vichy le 10 juillet 1940," *Revue d'histoire moderne et contemporaine*, 38 (October–December 1991), 563.
17. Andrew Shennan, *The Fall of France, 1940* (London, 2000), 117; Olivier Wieviorka, *Les Orphelins de la République. Destinées des députés et sénateurs français (1940–1945)* (Paris, 2001), 195.
18. Wieviorka, *Orphelins de la République*, 328–32, 336, 350.
19. Paxton's exact words are: "The Battle of France from the French side was a bit like one of those nightmares of slow-motion emergency in which one knows exactly what needs to be done but moves with agonizing slowness." Idem, *Europe in the Twentieth Century* (New York, 1975), 441.

Conclusion: The 1940 Syndrome

1. I have borrowed the phrase from Robert Frank[enstein], "The Second World War through French and British Eyes," in Robert Tombs and Emile Chabal, eds, *Britain and France in Two World Wars: Truth, Myth and Memory* (London, 2013), 182.
2. Hence the title of Ernest May's book, *Strange Victory: Hitler's Conquest of France* (New York, 2000).

3. Hugh Frey, "Rebuilding France: Gaullist Historiography, the Rise-Fall Myth and French Identity (1945–58)," in Stefan Berger, Mark Donovan, and Kevin Passmore, eds, *Writing National Histories: Western Europe Since 1800* (London, 1999), 205–16; Peter Jackson, "Post-War Politics and the Historiography of French Strategy and Diplomacy before the Second World War," *History Compass*, 4/5 (2006), 870–905.

4. This is not such a new point: see René Rémond and Janine Bourdin, eds, *Edouard Daladier, Chef de Gouvernement* (Paris, 1977); Elisabeth du Réau, *Edouard Daladier, 1884–1970* (Paris, 1993); and more recently Philip Nord, *France's New Deal: From the Thirties to the Postwar Era* (Princeton, NJ, 2010).

5. Robert Frank[enstein], *La Hantise du déclin. Le rang de la France en Europe, 1920–1960: finances, défense et identité nationale* (Paris, 1994), 255; Pierre Laborie, *L'Opinion française sous Vichy* (Paris, 1990), 239; H. Roderick Kedward, "Patriots and Patriotism in Vichy France," *Transactions of the Royal Historical Society*, 32 (1982), 191.

6. Serge Klarsfeld, *Vichy-Auschwitz: La 'solution' finale de la question juive en France* (Paris, 2001), vol. I, 11.

7. Laborie writes of the French public's general "non-consent." See *Le Chagrin et le venin. La France sous l'Occupation, mémoires et idées reçues* (Paris, 2011), 208.

8. See Jacques Semelin, *Face au totalitarisme, la résistance civile* (Paris, 2011); idem, *Sans Armes face à Hitler, 1939–1945: La Résistance civile en Europe* (Paris, 2013); idem, *Persécutions et entraides dans la France occupée. Comment 75% des Juifs en France ont échappé à la mort* (Paris, 2013); François Marcot, "Pour une sociologie de la Résistance: intentionnalité et fonctionnalité," in Antoine Prost, ed., *La Résistance, une histoire sociale* (Paris, 1997), 23, 26; and Claire Andrieu, "Sauvetages dans l'Europe allemande," unpublished ms. My special thanks to the author for permitting me to cite from her work.

9. Cited in Hanna Diamond, *Fleeing Hitler: France 1940* (London, 2007), 193.

10. Olivier Wieviorka, *Les Orphelins de la République. Destinées des députés et sénateurs français (1940–1945)* (Paris, 2001), 311.

INDEX